AMSTERDAM
Red Light District

'The Wallen'

The future of our past

Mariska Majoor

Photography by Robin Haurissa

Colophon

Text: Mariska Majoor

Photography: Robin Haurissa

Editing Dutch: Sylvia Emonts

Editing and translation: Petra Timmermans

Layout and design: Henk Kulk / ReproDesign

Published by De Wallenwinkel.

www.dewallenwinkel.nl

© Amsterdam, February 2023

All rights reserved. No part of this publication may be reproduced or stored in an automated data file and/or made public by print, photocopy, microfilm, e-document or by any other means without the express written permission of the publisher.

"It's a Sunday morning in the summer of 1995 and I am lying in bed listening to the church bells ringing from the Oude Kerk. The deep, reverberating tones bring up feelings of nostalgia. I don't know if that's youthful sentiment, leftover from my catholic upbringing, or because I just really love the sound of the enormous bells calling parishioners to mass. What I do know is that I have no desire to get out of bed. On more than one occasion during the night a window prostitute set off the alarm in her room. Once it even escalated into a brawl between a group of African women and a man in his underpants. I was able to follow it all from my bedroom window. The woman, who the half-naked man had a problem with, ran after him with a broom in her hand all the while hurling incomprehensible curses at him. Always ready for a fight, her colleagues quickly came to her defence. In the end he ran across the Oudekerksplein with his clothing in hand and his shoes flying through the air after him. I felt a little sorry for him and suspected he was feeling both frightened and ashamed at being seen nearly naked in this still rather controversial neighbourhood".

A little history

Whenever I am on the Oudekerksplein, I can always clearly imagine the Wallen of the past. Almost every stone breathes history in this neighbourhood. There are some beautiful books written about the founding of Amsterdam and more specifically about the history of the Wallen. Books put together by people with a lot of historical knowledge and who are able to write in such wonderful detail. I wouldn't even dream of trying to achieve something similar. In this book I just want to shed a little light on its history. This small piece of old Amsterdam – and here I limit myself to the neighbourhood within the old city walls known internationally as Amsterdam's 'Red Light District' – which occupies an area of less than one square kilometre. The Wallen is bordered by the Warmoesstraat, the Geldersekade, part of the Kloveniersburgwal and – to complete the circle – the Oude Hoogstraat and the Damstraat.

The Wallen has been fundamental to forming Amsterdam's identity, and from its earliest days it has also been the cause of much discussion. Here in and around this square lie the roots of Amsterdam, deeply anchored in the heart of our capital city and invisibly interwoven with the remains of those Amsterdammers who found their final resting place in the graveyard next to the old church, the Oude Kerk. In the late middle ages, these church grounds were seen as a sort of sanctuary; a place in the city where one might ignore governmental rules. While the dead found their permanent rest here, the ladies of easy virtue could also take a break among the headstones or see to their clients' needs; earning a little money without risk of being caught by the magistrate. Of course these activities were a thorn in the eye of many good citizens. Around 1413, a legal prohibition on immoral activities in graveyards put an end to this kind of thing. Although window prostitution around the Oude Kerk exists for only a century or so, prostitution has been practised here since the earliest days of the city. And just as today, it was always a topic of discussion which resulted in changes in policy and law. This whole neighbourhood has been regarded as a 'safe space' for free expression for a very long time, although what that meant and how it manifested has changed over time. It was not so much a place without any rules, but as the Wallen; one small part of Amsterdam where you could be free to be who you were. Where you could think freely. Where you could be just a little bit rebellious. Although, there were those who thought it was where all the criminals gathered and made their own rules.

From the beginning, Amsterdam has had enormous appeal for people from all levels of society. This former farming village located on the river Amstel, grew to become an important port city with multicultural influences and a tolerance for activities that most people couldn't be public about. In particular, for those coming here after months of hard work and loneliness on the seas.

In every port city, wherever you go in the world, you will find pubs and (il)legal brothels. In the Wallen they remained, and the city has always been famous for this. In 1681, a book was published about: *'Amsterdam's whoredom', where in the night, men are led by the devil into pubs and dance halls and warns against 'the cunning and trickery used to profit the whores and madams there…'*

Even in those days people pointed to Amsterdam with reproach; the city of sin where evil reigned supreme. Within the city there was also opposition to the dance parlours, some of which had rooms above where 'the girls' would take clients they had picked up below for paid sex. However, with the city expanding, growing economic prosperity and perhaps even spurred on by social resistance, the number of brothels continued to grow. Religion and morality were united in the fight against moral decay and they were the obvious opponents to the dance parlours, pubs and later brothels. Periods where prostitution was forbidden alternated with moments when it was not only tolerated as a 'necessary evil', but even facilitated by government through city-run brothels.

Meanwhile, life went on 'as normal' and people worked hard in their various trades in the harbour, the village and later in the city surrounding the Oude Kerk. Many of the stone relief plaques throughout the area attest to this. Even in present-day Amsterdam, the Wallen remains a neighbourhood where people live and work. Some in professions that completely confirm Amsterdam's international image and for others not at all. In fact, the Wallen acts as a sort of moral compass. The socio-political developments in this area reveal the direction the city is heading. For me the neighbourhood acts as a mirror to society. As the world around us becomes more conservative and morality gains importance, public discussion automatically shifts focus to prostitution and sex businesses, but also drugs and alcohol. These activities are happening everywhere but take place openly in the Wallen, co-existing with everything else that life has to offer.

The current discussion about the future of the Wallen, and in particular window prostitution, is somewhat different than the nationwide uproar that led to the ban against brothels in 1911 (lifted again in 2000), but there are similarities. If it was left up to some political parties in city council, we would be turning the clock back a hundred years to a time when Amsterdam seriously cracked down on 'evil'. Legislating the ban against brothels was meant to restore morality. But as expected, new ways were found to do business.

For example, there were suddenly a suspicious number of cigar shops opening in the old city, some of which were clandestine brothels. A little later, the first window brothels appeared in an area called the Pijp and in the Wallen. As befitting free-thinking spaces, people turned a blind eye and the brothels were tolerated.

"It is 1984. I want to buy a dog. In the newspaper there is an advertisement for a four-month-old German shepherd. I fall in love at first sight when I go to see her. For her too. We are meant for each other. She costs two hundred and fifty guilders. I just turned sixteen, have run away from home and I am sleeping in a squatted building. My chance of finding a job isn't so great and I don't have two cents to rub together. After begging the owners to give me until the evening to get the money for her, I go and ask everyone I know for a loan, without luck. Then someone gives me the number of a brothel, a so-called private house. I call them and I'm told that I can start right away. What do I care, I think. That same evening after two one-hour client sessions, I have enough money to get my dog. I call her Santa".

In the Wallen

Towards the end of 2019 I am sitting with my daughter Robin on the steps in front of the PIC (Prostitution Information Centre) in the Enge Kerksteeg. We look out towards the Oudekerksplein. A British man is standing negotiating by one of the windows and then races around the corner and returns with his friend. Laughing they both disappear through the door. I sigh when I hear the house music, feeling somewhat melancholic. What a racket! Definitely very different from the Celia Cruz that older colleagues used to play there.

I look up at the bedroom window of what used to be my old apartment. From this vantage point I watched a whole world pass by, had interesting conversations, laughed and cried; often with complete strangers. This square will always have a place in my heart. I never came here when I used to work behind a window two canals further up. This area was where my African colleagues worked and it was made clear to me that I had no business here. In those days, each area of the Wallen formed its own small community with its own unique characteristics. That's changed somewhat over the years.

I became better acquainted with the Oudekerksplein in 1994 when I opened the PIC. At that time it was mostly Latina women working there during the day. I will never forget the image of the Dominican sex workers sweeping the street in front of their windows at nine in the morning, singing their cheerful music together and chatting in what for me was an incomprehensible language. When a man walked by, one of them would call out to him 'I love you pappie!' and then they would all burst out laughing. They would sprinkle the stoop royally with ammonia in order to guarantee a good day, and sometimes the fire alarm would go off from the smoke from their giant cigars. That could be the image today if city officials and police were not required to make sure that the women kept the door to their window shut and didn't come out on the street in their work clothes. Not even if that is just to visit a friend two doors further up for a coffee. Sprinkling ammonia is forbidden and the music can't be too loud. They are not allowed to do anything anymore. The playfulness and unique culture of window prostitution is being stamped out by local regulations.

I moved into an apartment above the PIC. From day one I had spats with my famous neighbour Tante (Auntie) Mien. I thought it would be fun to organise a barbecue together with the new neighbours in the Enge Kerksteeg. It turned out it wasn't such a good plan. Tante Mien held onto some rather conservative views when it came to the Wallen. She lived above the window where she had worked as a prostitute when she was younger. Her reaction was to yell from her window: "Get lost! On this square you work, not barbecue"! This was not our last conflict. I think it was around fifteen years before we were able to greet each other normally. If you want to learn more about this fascinating character I recommend watching the documentary 'Rondom het Oudekerksplein (1968)'.

In 2016 I became seriously ill and said goodbye to the PIC. I miss it a lot but I miss these steps the most. It seems that I said that out loud. "I do too actually," echoes Robin. "I also sat here a lot, but it took a long time before I was allowed to sit here by myself". That's true. I may love this neighbourhood, but there are hordes of idiots and randy men walking around. Letting a young, pretty girl sit alone on the doorstep was only asking for trouble. Because of that there was always someone who kept an eye on her. I look at her and I have so many questions. What was it like for Robin to hang around here and then talk about how she spent her time when she was at school the next day? Was she colourfully descriptive about her mother's work, and her own experiences of an environment with condoms and women in bikinis standing behind the windows?

I ask Robin: "Can you remember what you thought when you were a child about what you saw happening around you here, a sort of first memory?" "No, not really," Robin answers. "It's the same if you asked me what my first memory of our house was. For me it was just there. It was always there and it felt really normal. I can remember moments. Like when I went with you and we entered the Warmoesstraat from the Damrak, through the Oude Brugsteeg. The first thing you saw then was that giant sign with a sexy woman above the sex shop Chickita's. I knew when I saw that sign that we were there. That was my landmark. I did notice that there were also a lot of weirdos around, but I have never felt uncomfortable in this neighbourhood".

"When did you realise what was happening behind the windows and what prostitution actually was," I ask. "That happened little by little" Robin answers, "You always talked about selling kisses and I just accepted that. Kind of: oh okay. I didn't think that was crazy and it was really clear. The windows do draw your attention though if you walk through the area. I didn't dare to really look, but you always said: "Just be normal. You are allowed to look, but just be nice, like you are with everyone else. And if you know someone, just wave or something". I understood that it was work. They sell kisses. They sell something, so that's work. Just the same, I also wondered about all kinds of things".

I never wanted to keep Robin away from the Wallen or hide sex work from her. It wouldn't have been possible anyway. It is an important and public part of my life. I have asked myself whether or not I have made things more difficult for her by being so easygoing about it. I also didn't want her to be treated badly by other people because of my work and my past.

A lot of women with children, who are working in sex work, keep it secret for their entire lives. I would prefer if secrecy wasn't necessary, but society isn't as tolerant as it seems and we want to protect our children. Robin says that things were not difficult for her. And to my surprise she says that it was actually an important benefit to her upbringing.

We sit silently and listen to the church bells. They ring every quarter hour. There are quite a lot of people passing by, but the atmosphere is relaxed. Most people stroll quietly across the square looking around, their eyes travelling from window brothel to church tower. If the complaints about how crazy busy it is are true, it's not noticeable at the moment. Not yet.

Negative reactions come mainly from other women. I hear some making really cruel and degrading comments as they walk past a window where someone is standing. An English-speaking woman yells out: "Oh my god, that's terrifying!" I have to bite my tongue. Various people take photos of a window prostitute, some while standing directly in front. If someone says something about it, they act surprised.

"It is 1985 and probably a Saturday night. Hordes of people pass by my window on the Oudezijds Achterburgwal. They don't interest me. I scan the crowd looking for potential clients. Suddenly a bright light flashes. Someone takes a photo. Furious, I wrench the door open and run after the photographer along with my high-heeled colleagues. He stands frozen with his camera and its enormous flash balanced on his belly, waiting to see what happens. The crowd lets us through and watches with bated breath. I grab the camera, open it, and I rip out the roll of film. 'Don't ever do that again' I snap at him, tossing the roll with a wide arc into the canal. The photographer doesn't know what hit him and doesn't dare protest. Better for him because our boyfriends are running across the bridge toward us. We don't need them, we can take care of this ourselves. We head back to our windows laughing and a bit hyper, having no idea about the possibilities people will have in twenty years with their digital cameras and smartphones".

Nigel, the window washer, comes and stands near us and rolls a cigarette. "Not much has changed, has it" I sigh, as we watch a group of older Americans get an earful for standing in front of one of the windows for too long. "Nope" he says, "and I don't see that happening soon".

Nigel is a funny, cynical Scot who came to Amsterdam in the mid-eighties. We also both acted together in a German documentary about John Irving. Irving had just written a book partly taking place in a brothel in Amsterdam. When Nigel first came to Amsterdam he visited the Wallen for the 'entertainment', as he so nicely puts it. He saw it as a party town. Since 1990 he has been running his own window washing business and most of his clients are in the Wallen area. "You don't shit on your own doorstep", he says. "Since I have my business and now also a family, I am only here on a professional basis". There isn't a window in the Wallen that he doesn't know. "You've probably seen a lot from your ladder," I say to him. "Now", he laughs. "Actually, I've mostly heard a lot. The Wallen is kind of a school for me. I learn something new everyday". Nigel can talk up a storm, always has interesting anecdotes and he also has an opinion about everything. "I love the people and 'soap opera' of the street," he begins. "I should mention though that I am only here in the daytime.

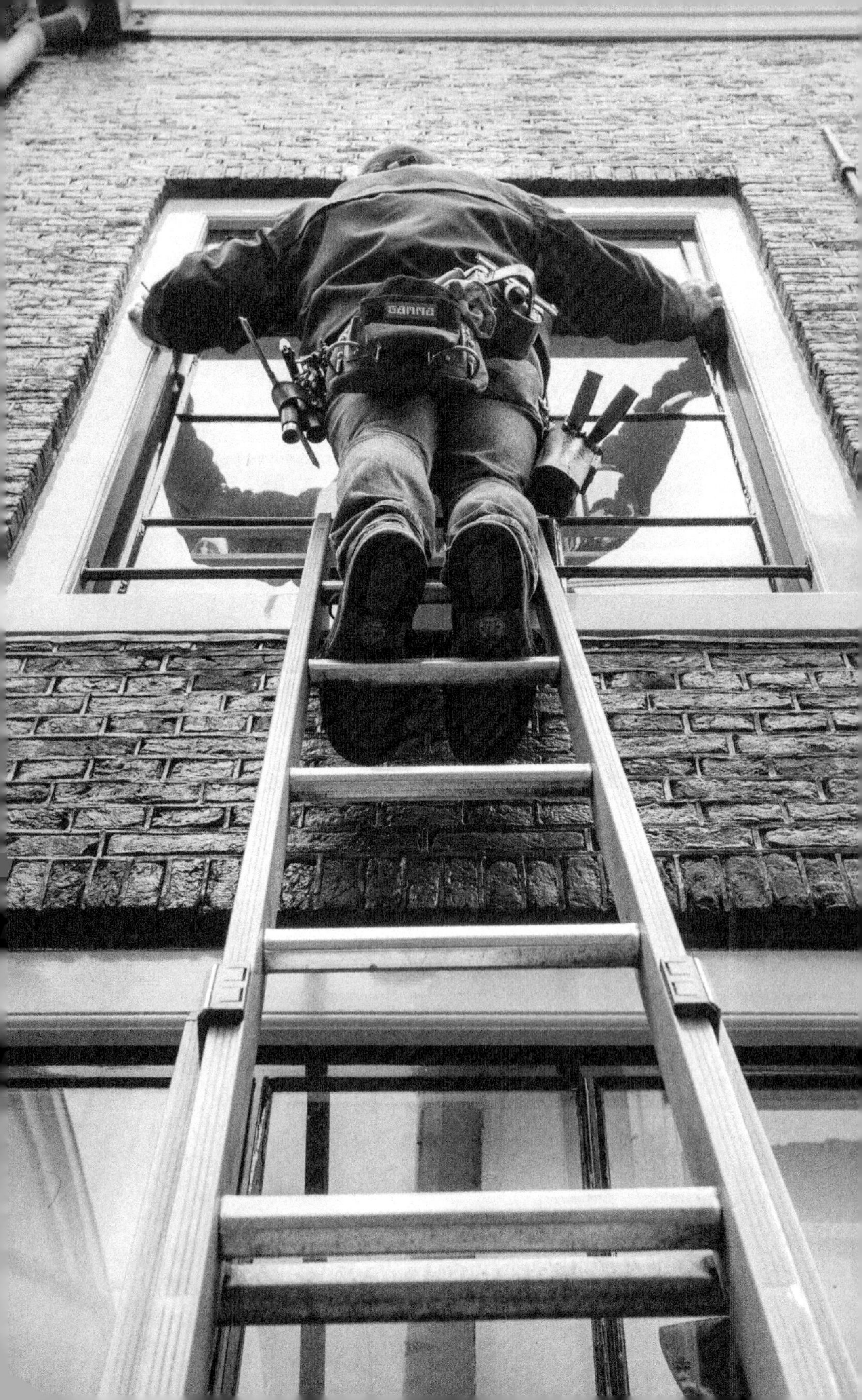
GAMMA

I don't have to deal with the Saturday night chaos and the problems that everyone complains about. I experience the Wallen as a well-organised neighbourhood. I never see criminality. My clients are cafes, gay shops, tattoo parlours, coffee shops, stores, window brothels and peoples' homes… in fact, everything you find in the neighbourhood. I have been coming by a lot of businesses for so long that I make my own coffee there. The things I learn about here range from the best butter for fisting - I'll spare you the details - to coffee machine brands and everything in between.

Ten years ago Lodewijk Asscher commented on the Wallen saying: 'There's a snake hiding under every stone'. I definitely don't feel that way about the neighbourhood. What I mostly see is people who work hard and who have always treated me well. The city forced a lot of window brothels to close. Tax-paying window prostitutes had to vacate for artists on subsidies and as soon as the subsidies stop, the artists disappear. I don't see the economic benefits of this. On top of that, they never cleaned their windows", Nigel says with a wink.

"I also don't understand closing the coffee shops and encouraging all the new pubs and restaurants. Everyone in the neighbourhood will tell you that the problem isn't with people who are stoned. It's actually the drunks who cause a lot of the nuisance. We've had plenty of discussions about this in Scotland. We know that if you put twelve men in a room with half drinking whiskey and half smoking a joint, that after an hour the stoned guys will be laughing their heads off and the drunks will be punching each other out. Also, the crazy bureaucratic regulations are really irritating. I spoke recently with a hard-working baker in the Warmoesstraat who told me that he had to get a permit for the plant that he had by his front door. What's that about? We don't need that kind of government interference, self-regulation is something that still exists".

That reminds me of the time the city sent me a warning letter too because of a dress I had hung from the door of Rood, my store in the Warmoesstraat. The letter said that the dress ruined the 'character' of the street and threatened a thousand euro fine if I did it again. "There has been a shift in the neighbourhood from organic to organised pleasure," Nigel adds. "Disneyland-style fun. The Wallen may have been less legally regulated in the old days, but there was a great deal of community control. Now rules are determined externally, by people who know nothing of the neighbourhood. They don't know how and what they need to regulate. I was shocked when I saw a Domino's Pizza on the Lange Niezel street. Until recently there were really a lot of small businesses in the Wallen. Now the big chain franchises that we see everywhere, are coming into this area too. It has fundamentally changed this once unique neighbourhood. I wonder why you would want that".

Nigel's cigarette is finished and he climbs up his ladder again. Ready to move on, we stand up and say our goodbyes. We turn left from the Enge Kersteeg onto the square and walk towards the Oudezijds Voorburgwal. I peek into the building next door to the PIC where the visitor's centre for the neighbourhood, called 'We Live Here', has recently located. A group of residents from the Wallen have organised, among other things, an exhibition featuring large-format portraits taken of people who live here sitting behind the windows of their homes. The objective is to show visitors that the Wallen is also a neighbourhood where people live and asks them to behave like they would at home. Of course, many tourists simply have no idea. I think explaining this could help.

For many years this building was home to a double window brothel, and for a long time it was Dominican Maria's workplace. She worked until she was seventy years old. The income that she earned in the Wallen supported the majority of her family. Maria told me that she had a house with a swimming pool in the Dominican Republic and she would go there a couple of times a year until she finally stopped working. Maria was a hard working, feisty woman who didn't give a damn about her age, but because of this had to put up with people's comments and ridicule every day. Usually from young people, who don't realise that one day – if they are lucky – they'll be old too.

People still work in the window brothel where Tante Mien once worked. I can't help but look up and imagine her hanging out the window, with her teased, blond, cotton-candy hair piled high on her head and her yelling at me to go to hell with my barbecue. Still, she has my respect.

Next door in an inner courtyard reached by a small alley there were also window brothels, but they disappeared already a few years ago. Bought out by the city. On the street side, a former window space is now occupied by the radio station, Red Light Radio. Although it's nice, it's also a painful example of how window prostitution has had to make way for other businesses, which then flirt with the red light image that was so necessary to get rid of.

> "It is 1996. My second-floor bedroom is on the Oudekerksplein side. On Friday and Saturday nights it's always party time on the streets, especially in the summer. I'm a light sleeper. If someone farts on the street, I wake up. So you can understand why I am up most weekend nights. The upstairs neighbours have less of a noise problem because their bedroom is to the back of the building. Mornings I go to 'wake up' at the Stones cafe on the square with a game of pool and a cappuccino. If it's sunny, I take a second coffee with me and go sit on my front steps. The mornings are nice and quiet. Only the street cleaners cleaning up the mess from the night before are making noise. Do I want to keep living here? Sure, at least for now, but I have plenty to complain about. Every morning my planters are full of trash and the little tree keeps getting pulled out by dealers who hide their stash there. I choose plants with all this in mind. They have to be able to take the abuse. People make noise, and yes, the tourist groups can be extremely irritating if you can't get through the streets. But then, it is the city and not the countryside. Plus I do enjoy a bit of action".

A new, modern sex cinema called 5Dporn recently opened in the next building, where the old Venus sex cinema used to be. Yes! I think to myself, it's so good that it didn't turn into a souvenir shop or a hipster cafe, where only the name reminds us of what used to be there. Up until it closed, the Venus was the only place in Amsterdam that still showed eight millimetre films from the seventies. Black and white images, pretty tame and with lots of body hair. A few sex workers who didn't have a window to work from would go there sometimes with a client. The cinema wasn't intended to be a place for sexual services, but you understand how these things go. Because of this, bringing a towel with you to cover the seat was no frivolous luxury. It was the end of an era when the Venus closed. The internet has been the main cause behind the decline of sex cinemas. When Robin was still young and began to play around on the computer, I was very alert about what images she was being exposed to. Children and sex don't go together. Even when sex is your work, that doesn't mean that you allow your children to come into unlimited contact with the subject. In fact, I am pretty prudish and I don't talk as easily about sex as you might imagine from someone who has been occupied with nothing else for most of her life. Given that, it is a pretty big thing to go into this sex cinema together with my daughter. Robin finds it just as awkward, but we do it anyway. We want to know what this 5D porn is all about. We watch what is a funny, short film about the neighbourhood. There are some pornographic elements but you'll miss them if you blink. The gyrating cinema seats feel like you are sitting on a roller-coaster and when there is an orgasm in the film, water mist and foam blows out over you from somewhere. With a straight face we watch the images on the screen, laughing as we experience the hysterical foam orgasm. We are in a good mood when it's over and we head back outside, walking straight into the arms of Laurens Buijs.

Project 1012

Laurens has been around the Wallen a lot in recent years. That's pretty remarkable for someone from provincial Limburg, who wanted to move to a larger urban area 12 years ago and ended up in Leiden because he found Amsterdam still a bit too overwhelming. "I was so naive then", Laurens says with a laugh. We continue walking on together as he talks more about his student years. "I was twenty-four and wanted to study sociology and political science. Really, I wanted to come to the big city, but I didn't dare to. I still hadn't come out of the closet and doing everything at the same time felt overwhelming. I fell instantly in love with Amsterdam once I did come, especially with the Wallen. Here everything God created and prohibited is all jumbled up together. I loved it". Laurens knows all about the changes in the Wallen in recent years. I asked him to talk about that.

"In 2007, the city began it's so called 'clean up the Red Light District' initiative; named 'Project 1012' for the postal area. At that time I was teaching a group of Political Science students who were looking for a research topic. I had just seen the launch of Project 1012 on TV and it really surprised me. The announced plans that were being discussed seemed like a complete departure from how things had always been done in the Wallen. Suddenly, a totally different narrative was being presented to the public. They were saying that everything was 'out of control' and that it was so dangerous there. This new narrative focussed on trafficking and injustice. It really surprised me that people weren't talking about this anywhere else in the city. As a political scientist that's very interesting. My reaction was that I needed to protest against these new plans. They made it seem that there was complete consensus. My gut feeling was that were some very clever power games happening. It raises questions when you are able to get such a broad proposal, with so much money and interests involved, accepted so easily by city council and public opinion. If all the city officials are in support, the money tap is turned on, and even the press eats it up, then you are doing something right and something interesting is going on. I was immediately aware of that. How it was framed was just so polished.

The people behind Project 1012 used emotionally charged messaging in order to win favour. The actual interests remained hidden. 'Safety' was emphasised and it was about combatting criminality and tax evasion. And most importantly: they wanted to save the women. A picture developed that women in the Wallen were victims of the most horrific forms of trafficking. Prostitution in the Wallen was equated with this. That could be corrected by implementing an urban planning approach. The problems could be solved by reducing the size of the area and getting rid of the rotten apples. As soon as I heard that, I immediately had a feeling: that picture makes no sense.

I recognised from the manner Project 1012 was launched and the kind of politician supporting it, a trend found in political literature. This was Neoliberalism, a new form of politics that wants to achieve its goals through market forces. It was immediately obvious to me: behind this project was money.

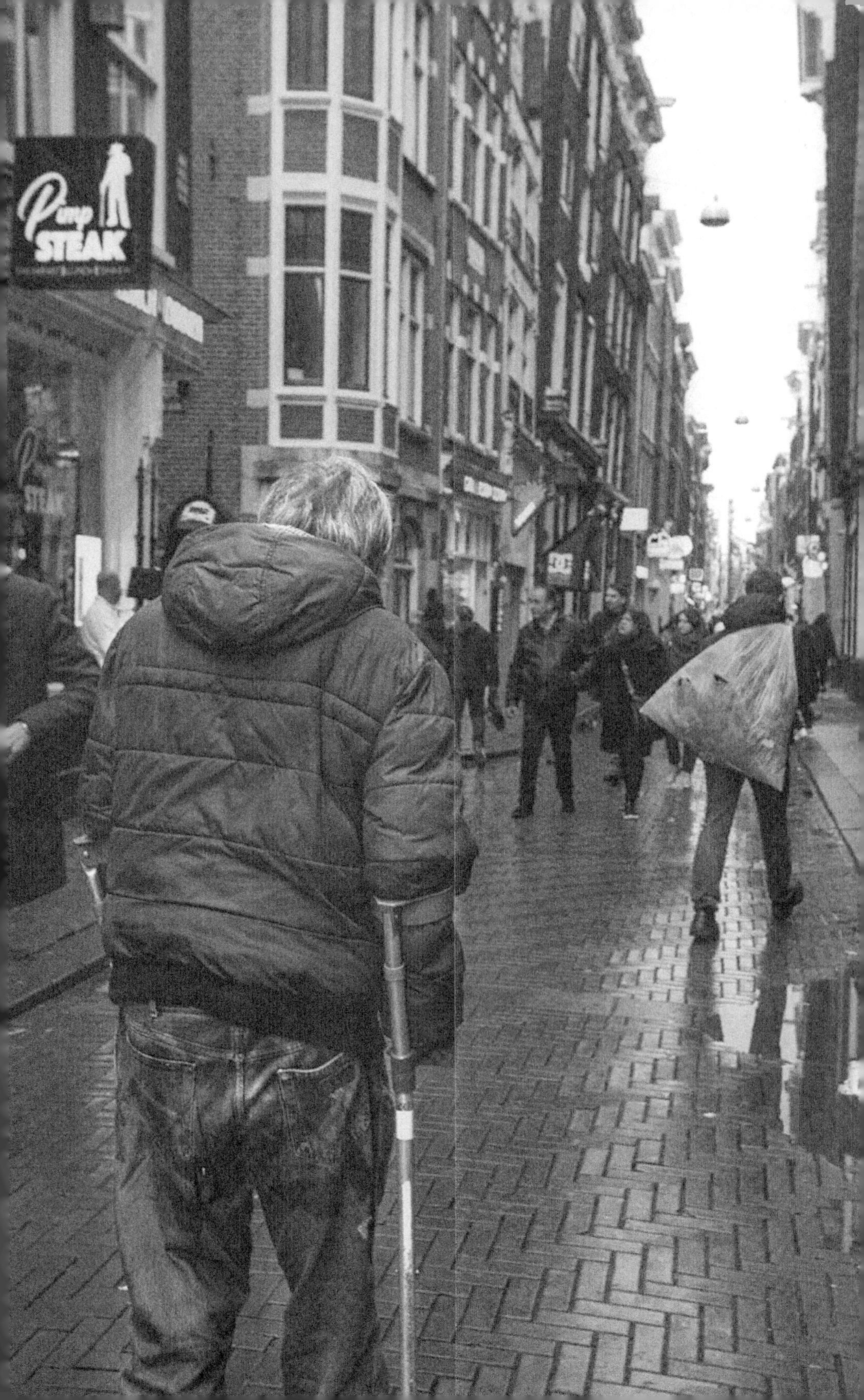
STEAK

Business is behind this; property transactions taking priority and shaping opinion about what the neighbourhood should look like. That was the actual goal of the project, which no one discussed, but was so obvious in how it had been set up. As a social scientist, I understand how unique the network operating in the Wallen is. By network, I mean the combination of business owners, residents, institutions, structures and functions that have developed there historically. Wow! Everything that is exciting to a researcher is there. There is cohesion, there is history, there is identity and authenticity. It is such a unique and precious piece of social fabric. By the way, that doesn't mean that I think everything is good: I am not talking about good or bad.

Project 1012 has destroyed that social fabric. It has been shredded. Very little attention has been paid to what makes the Wallen unique. It's as if a bulldozer has run over it. The city council doesn't see this as a mistake and that is so frustrating. They still don't see it. They have a 'checklist' mentality where they probably think that a lot of the goals have been achieved and tick items off a list. They look to where regulations have been implemented, where a garbage bin has been placed, where new uses have been located. They don't see the Wallen as a neighbourhood with a soul, as something that is alive. They have reduced the area to a program of policy goals and there is something not quite right about that. That's scary.

In many ways the fate of the Wallen is already determined. Zoning plans have been rushed through city council and the Council of State. There are land-use and financial commitments that have been in place for ten years already. The current mayor, Mayor Halsema, has presented four possible scenarios that are being discussed at this time. It's clear to me that not one of the four scenarios is based on the authentic social structure of the Wallen. It seems as if the city is saying: 'we are keeping all options open', but in practice it's business as usual, continuing on as it has been for the last ten years. Slowly creeping in the direction the planning department has always intended. You notice in everything that they are not yet resting on their laurels. They haven't realised their goals yet. I find it strange how suddenly people are talking in nature metaphors. Out of the blue the neighbourhood is a 'jungle' and needs to transform into a beautiful 'courtyard garden'.

And what's next? Well, I already feel that the neighbourhood has changed so much. It's still the Wallen but it's really taken a beating. The neighbourhood is centuries-old and has always been in the line of fire. In a certain way that's also what has shaped its identity. It's like Calimero: us against the world".

Feeling a little deflated we say goodbye to Laurens and walk further to the canal, where we order some French fries at the Febo on the other side and talk things over. I myself have experienced the period around Project 1012 as painful and hurtful. Someone like Lodewijk Asscher, who describes prostitution as commercial rape, can still keep me awake at night. This negative conceptualisation of the neighbourhood and it's people feels really unjust and Laurens' insights confirm that. How can individuals and communities defend their interests against politicians with a double agenda?

> "It is 2011. Lodewijk Asscher has been busy influencing public opinion about the Wallen again. Language is his latest weapon; using terms like 'commercial rape' for sex work and calling sex work rights activists 'armchair feminists'. I am furious with him. Yesterday evening I was interviewed by the BBC and they informed me that Asscher is hosting a media lunch today in the recently, and with much fanfare, opened (in the meantime already closed) flagship of Project 1012: restaurant Anna. There's no way that I can let this opportunity pass. I craft a gift certificate for a 'free workshop behind the window' and take it with me into the restaurant. Immediately the BBC and their cameras come and stand by me. For a split-second I ask myself what I'm doing here all alone. It probably comes off a bit clumsy, but if you start something then you should to see it through. I invite Asscher to come forward and I give him the gift certificate 'in the hope that it will help him to better understand what is really happening in the Wallen and he learns to be more respectful regarding sex workers." Asscher, aware that there are cameras on him, accepts the certificate with a laugh. He has never used it..."

"I notice that a lot of young people around me have been raised with the idea that prostitution is the same as trafficking," says Robin. "They assume that everyone who does this work is forced to do it one way or another. I was in middle school in the Project 1012 period and I heard this a lot then. If it was about the Wallen it was always linked to pimps and so-called lover boys. People say these things without knowing anyone who does this work. Because of you I know a lot of sex workers, so I think that it's okay for me to have an opinion. Even so, people often don't believe me when I try to tell them that there really is another side".

I gaze out to the other side of the canal. From here you see the back of the Oude Kerk. The window brothels on the corner are all occupied. The Ouderkerksplein has the highest occupancy rate of the Wallen. I think about my African colleagues who worked there twenty years ago and how there are so few still working in Amsterdam now. Most came here from Ghana and Nigeria. My contact with them was mostly superficial. I got to know a few better, but they didn't come into the PIC very often. Sometimes we chatted when I was sitting on the steps and they were on their way to work. 1994 was a beautiful summer. Sitting on the square with his easel, my father painted some of their portraits as they stood behind the window. This made for some hilarious scenes: women in lingerie who went up to him and made comments if the painting didn't resemble them. These were his first interactions with sex workers and it helped him in a really unique way in being able to process what his daughter was doing, and her past.

There were moments when wild stories circulated about how some of the African women arrived here. That's always been difficult for me. You are standing right on top of things but don't notice anything. What's true and what's not?

In 2018, Robin travelled to Nigeria together with sex worker rights activist Yvette Luhrs, where they spoke with sex workers there. They talked about colleagues fleeing poverty and a hopeless future by often willingly and knowingly putting their lives into the hands of traffickers. They hoped that they would earn money in Europe. This is difficult for us to imagine coming from a position of privilege in a wealthy country such as ours, but it is important to understand this or to at least try to understand.

With so much poverty in the world there are countless criminals who profit from the vulnerability of others; people who have nothing and who are willing to make drastic choices to save their families from hunger and poverty. We see a person in this situation in the Wallen as a victim. And maybe she is but a victim of what? Poverty and not prostitution is the problem because it makes people vulnerable to trafficking. There should be more focus on combating poverty instead of prostitution. In an honest world, without hunger and with equal rights and good labour conditions for everyone, poverty and prostitution would no longer be a problem.

> "It is 1992. I have started a small magazine about prostitution and I am in Friesland looking for brothels. I go into a shabby looking sex shop to ask if they know anything. Sex shops and taxi drivers are the best sources of information about this kind of thing. While I am talking with the owner about where I can find certain countryside brothels (seksboerderijen), I see a half open curtain behind the counter. There is a room there and I see a couple of women sitting. They are barely clothed and they look at me with suspicion. Hmm, what's going on here, I wonder. With a 'like knows like' smile I ask what kind of excitement happens behind the curtain and if I can look. My question crosses a line and as his friendly demeanour fades, he moves to the curtain to pull it closed. 'They are illegal Brazilians', he says. 'They won't understand you and you never saw them'. He makes it clear that I should leave. Later it turns out to be common knowledge and I am not sure at who or what I should be angry at".

Leaving the Febo we head over the bridge. I know it as the 'pill bridge' (pillenbrug), although the original pillenbrug is closer to the Damstraat. True to its name all kinds of pills were offered for sale here, but that was only one of the many things available here in the open-air drug market. In the seventies and lasting for more than a decade the Zeedijk was the centre of the heroin trade in the Netherlands. The associated problems were enormous. By the mid-eighties the worst of it was over, but the problems persisted until well into the nineties. Dealers fanned out across many other streets and bridges in the area, including this one. You imagined that you were in the Bronx in New York instead of charming Amsterdam. The hippy scene, with its relatively harmless soft drugs, was replaced by Chinese mafia, Surinamese dealers and heroin addicts that were dropping like flies. I experienced all this only peripherally. Heroin was never my thing, but I knew this bridge well. A lot of hustling and drug-dealing happened here. The scarce and easily intimidated tourists, given the character of the neighbourhood, were better off avoiding the area. Hanging out on the bridge to take photos, like tourist do these days, was not an option.

Clients were taken to a cheap by-the-hour hotel up the street or serviced in the dark allies, several of which have since been closed off by high fences. If a junkie had just gone into one to shoot up, you just went one alley further. Photographer Gerard Wessel made an incredible photo series with raw images of the junkies that were characteristic of this neighbourhood at that time. Was it a mess? Yes. Was what was happening nice? No. But it wasn't fake; it was real.

Hustling on the bridge declined sharply after the cheap, by-the-hour hotels were shut down and there was a crackdown on street prostitution. The drug issue was dealt with using different strategies. By street 'sweeps', which really meant chasing dealers and users so that they didn't hang out long in any one place, the forced incarceration of addicts with psychiatric problems in closed institutions and by establishing rehabilitation and other support programs. The changed drug scene and further improvements to the neighbourhood saw to it that this part of the Wallen isn't like that anymore. It is clean, it is safe and it is beautiful. But it is also very prim and proper. It's almost 'normal' here. I miss the rough edges.

People who live on the fringes of society are generally no angels, but I often find them to be interesting characters. They have stories to tell and there is a lot of creativity. You find poets, painters and bon vivants. People who live off the beaten track add character to the neighbourhoods where they stay. Start disturbing the area and they feel out of place and shy away. Of course, that is the objective of a city renewal project. But where do you go if you don't fit in anywhere and refuse to be warehoused in a shelter?

I have always been sensitive to the energy in so-called bad neighbourhoods. I greedily seek out places where people are authentic and not just keeping up appearances, and where I can feel that life is being lived. Perhaps that's why I sometimes secretly and longingly look back to the time before the big clean-up began, and before the people who lived in the middle of it all were swept out of sight along with the filth and drugs of the street.

Sonja totally gets it when I mention it to her. She hustled on and around this bridge for years. At just eighteen Sonja left her prescription drug addicted mother and has never seen her since. She first worked for a couple of years in an after hours cafe in the Haarlemmerstraat. That's where she first came into contact with hard drugs. Prior to that she hadn't even smoked a joint. "I'm a pleaser," Sonja says. "That happens when you've never felt loved. As soon as someone is nice to me, my inclination is to do anything for them. I was homeless and the boss of the cafe let me sleep upstairs. But he also pushed me to work hard and I was always exhausted. You could get anything in that cafe. At some point someone gave me a packet of coke. And wow, I really loved it. I suddenly felt like I could handle everything again. I started using more and more, eventually heroin too. Every time a step further. The cafe was raided and I was jailed for a month, but as soon as I was out the drugs started calling me again. I hadn't been able to kick the habit in the month that I was away.

It wasn't long after that I ended up in the Wallen. In those days it was easy for me to get money and drugs there. I mainly hustled on the Geldersekade, but also behind Central Station or here on this bridge sometimes. I learned how to go about business from dealers. Especially how I could drug tourists and then steal from them. They told me that they would protect me for a cut of the money. In the beginning that was pretty scary, but the drugs were the only thing important to me so I didn't really think about it much. It didn't take me long to figure out that I could do all of this myself. Junkies are greedy, you don't want to share because you need it for yourself. When you're an addict and sick you're not very critical because you need drugs. At that moment anything will do.

Since I was still homeless I was also really vulnerable. Doing something for five guilders was nothing. There are guys who learn to recognise when you are sick and wait for their moment. Some would buy methadone on the pillenbrug by the Damstraat.

If they saw someone who was symptomatic – convulsing or looking grey – they would offer pills if you did something for them first. When you have withdrawal symptoms, you are willing to do things that even a dog would turn its nose up at. So yeah, that's the way it was. I didn't know anything about the cheap trick hotels here. I didn't have a lot of street smarts and I was pretty naive. I hustled everywhere although mostly in cars. A lot of the men were like those guys that used to go around with a cart scavenging scrap metal; older and grubby. As strange as it sounds, they often reminded me of my mother.

Working on the street isn't very nice you know. It's cleaner and safer indoors. I can't imagine someone who isn't addicted or in survival mode choosing to work on the street. It's especially dangerous if you go outside of the neighbourhood. I ended up getting raped by four men because I left the Wallen with someone in a car. I never wanted to hustle again after that. Easily said, but what are you going to do then to get money for drugs? I bought Rohypnol on the bridge - what we called roofies - and would try to get a drunk tourist to go for a cup of coffee. The pills disintegrate best in coffee. If that worked I took him to a sex shop where they had movie booths. Once I got him into a booth, I would wait until he was 'out' and could steal his stuff. I was never caught and I was very efficient. Every six hours I needed a fix, I was very disciplined about that. These days I am off of everything except methadone and Valium. I have my own home and still receive mentoring support. For a long time now I have been volunteering at the Rainbow Group's homeless shelter and I give talks about the Wallen. I am really open about my past. I am glad that it's in the past, but I'm also still happy that I experienced it all. I have no regrets, it's only a pity that it lasted so long and cost me so much. For twenty five years I lived with addiction and I am only just now starting to live a normal life".

I look at Sonja and try to imagine her the way she was then. It must have been such a difficult time. I feel sorry for the drunk tourists that she fleeced, but find her description of the 'scrap metal scavengers' disgusting.

From the bridge we look out on one of the oldest stone-built houses in Amsterdam. The Salvation Army is using it and it's also where Major Bosshardt had her office. In this neighbourhood the Salvation Army does a lot for the homeless and addicted. They have always had enough to do here and are able to provide support to many women such as Sonja. Fortunately she is doing well, and these days the tourists that she meets are in safe and caring hands.

"There are a lot of dealers in the area again at the moment, but not as many as there used to be. Back then a big horn hung outside here by the Febo," Sonja continues. "All kinds of things happened on the pavement but inside too. Sometimes you could get your drugs along with your chicken snack from the self-serve vending wall. The Febo had nothing to do with that of course. Dealers are just smart at hiding their drugs. If things got to be too much or too dangerous, someone would blow the horn and then everyone ran off in all directions. In comparison, it's pretty boring on the street now. There was always something going on in the past and it was not without danger. Still, I have always felt safe in the Wallen. No one from outside of my little circle wanted anything to do with me because I was 'just a heroin whore'. This neighbourhood felt like home to me. In those years, I could wander peacefully along the Zeedijk. It was outside of the area that I was scared and self-conscious.

On the street here, I would often bump into the African girls from the the church who wanted to pray with me. I thought that was beautiful. They weren't embarrassed by me. I have absolutely no problem talking about my experiences and I want to explain things. Some young people are really cocky about using drugs. I hope that once they have heard my story, they will think differently about it. People see me as a drug addiction survivor. But I want to be more than that. What I really want is for people to see me as worthy. I am more than the things I have done."

Sonja gets on her scooter and carefully rides off. She thinks Amsterdammers are anti-social towards tourists, who are terrified by the crazy bike and scooter culture here, so she avoids doing that. The way she used to treat tourists had to do with her addiction and not her as a person. Now that she's pretty much clean, her true self is resurfacing and that is really nice to see. Robin and I stay a moment longer to take in the surroundings. The view to the Sint Nicolaaskerk (Saint Nicholas Church), foregrounded by centuries-old buildings at the top of the Zeedijk, is stunning. It is often photographed by the groups of tourists standing on the bridge. Most are unaware of everything that's happened here on this spot. Right in front of us are two young, clean-cut men looking around for something. "We want to go to the Chinese area," they hesitantly answer when I ask if I can help them. "Well, you are in the Wallen now," I tell them and I have to laugh when I see how they are a bit startled to hear this. I show them on their way and find it interesting that in this day and age two young men have no idea where they are. Or were they just good actors?

> "It is 2013. I am giving a walking tour through the neighbourhood to a group of American students. They look around in amazement. At one end of the bridge we stand while I tell them a few things. They really do try to listen to what I am saying, but so many other things are demanding their attention. Now and then they nod their heads. These students come from a country where prostitution is illegal and if they do see it there, then it's often people with addictions. That's what has shaped their ideas about prostitution and what makes it all hard for them to take in. They aren't used to talking openly about sex either, so if you find that difficult then I can understand how prostitution is a few steps too far. Suddenly two tomcats come brawling out of a cafe and there is a lot of commotion. One cat is ginger and the other black. Everything moves really fast. Before we know it the black cat falls a couple of meters into the canal. The ginger cat takes a look at him, thinks: good riddance, and walks back to the cafe again. The black cat makes a frantic effort to keep its head above water and is thrashing its way along the much too high canal walls. There is no way he can get out by himself. Everyone stands in shock at the bridge railing and the students are closer to crying than laughing. I run into the cafe and grab two construction workers from their barstools to help. A little further up the canal the wall is lower and there is a barge in the water there. Both men lay on their stomachs, one on the boat and one on the side of the canal. At the moment the cat paddles close enough, the man on the boat grabs it out of the water and hurls it up to the other guy, who dumps the dripping wet cat in my arms. Someone runs out of a nearby hotel with a towel. The students watch all this with bated breath and applaud. This is one visit to the Wallen they will certainly never forget".

Children in the Wallen

"Actually, how did you answer questions about the Wallen at school?" I asked Robin. "In elementary school it wasn't a problem," she answers. "Sometimes friends would even come with me, right? They found it really exciting. Coming to Amsterdam and 'your store', as we called it. We were also allowed to go and get French fries. Man in those days, I was the best 'after school playmate'. When I was twelve and in middle school it was completely different. I was more aware, so I would assess the situation before telling someone about the Wallen and your work. I didn't dare to be so open about that. Until my classmates discovered it for themselves online. The reactions were positive, so it wasn't that bad. Actually, people are always very interested. I wonder if that's because of the types of people around us or that maybe the negative stereotypes aren't as bad as we think.

People are always very curious about me and want to know everything. The one thing that could really make me mad, was when they used the word 'whore' as a curse word at school. I felt like it was a personal attack on you. There is always so much negativity in the media about sex work and the Wallen, that I was scared about the reactions. So when I went to a new school in Amsterdam, I kept it to myself in the beginning too. But also there it wasn't long before they found out, thanks to the internet."

We wave to Michel from the flower shop 'Jemi', who screeches up on his delivery bike. For the most part Michel grew up in the neighbourhood. When he was eleven, his parents moved right across from the notorious Warmoestraat police station. Classmates always wanted to go home with him just to hang out the window and watch everything that was happening on the street. If his parents went out for the evening they left him with Max, the downstairs neighbour in the sex shop. "Those evenings were always fun," Michel tells us when I ask him about his younger days in the neighbourhood. "Max made music cassettes for Radio Benidorm and he let me help him. My first job was at the hotel Kabul here in the Warmoestraat. I was the handyman's assistant and had to fix bar stools and toilets. I had a really great childhood here and wasn't really affected by the problems and trouble in the area. I played soccer on the Beursplein and had friends who lived by the Nieuwmarkt. There were some places you just didn't go, for example, the area behind the Nieuwmarkt and the Zeedijk. We stayed away from there. But it was really great in the Warmoesstraat. I think growing up in the Wallen has made me more flexible. The neighbourhood taught me how to get along with people and to not have prejudices. I have them of course but I deal with them differently. You learn to accept people for who they are. Still, some things do scare me. A few months ago I was threatened by a dealer who was high as a kite, and there was a stabbing murder recently. It takes a toll. Even though it happened much more often in the past. What's sad is that we were more used to it back then and it was almost 'normal'.

A few years ago there was a television series about the earlier days of the Zeedijk. It made me realise that I had no idea what all was happening there back then. When I saw it on the television I thought: what a tough neighbourhood it was and asked myself how my parents even dared to move here with two small children. It was my mother's dream to have a flower shop here with an apartment above it. None of us ever regretted it. We had a lot of trouble with junkies and dealers, but when you live here you experience these things very differently. If they were standing by the shop entrance we could just go up to them and say: 'come on guys, it's time to move somewhere else'. Then they'd say: 'Hey flower man' and move on without any further trouble. These days it's much more boring on the street, but also much more explosive. Especially heading into the weekend. The people on the street are different, they have a shorter fuse and the drugs are different. Maybe that's the reason. I think it's unfortunate and unnecessary that so many of the coffee shops are closed. We never went on vacation. There was so much to do here in the neighbourhood. There were restaurants from so many different cultures and everyone knew each other. It was really nice. There was a togetherness and that doesn't exist anymore.

The tourists can tire you out sometimes, but maybe that has more to with my age and the fact that I have been here so long. You are really forced to adjust your life when it's so busy around you. Even so, I would never want to move. It makes me happy that there are still a few crackpots wandering around here now and then. In the Warmoesstraat here, you can walk down the street in your pyjamas or butt naked and no one would think anything of it. If you lived in Aalsmeer people would think you were bonkers. Here it makes them happy. We could also be sitting in Sloterdijk to make our flower arrangements because what the shop sales bring in is nothing to write home about, but then we would miss all the fun. I don't even want to think about it".

In the Wallen of bygone days there were a lot of families with children living here – also next to the brothels – and they just played out on the street. Over time it became busier in the neighbourhood and the 'red light district' began to develop. Playing safely outside wasn't possible any longer. Many of the buildings in the Wallen are large and some have beautiful inner courtyards. The Princess Juliana nursery school on the Ouderkerksplein also has an outdoor play area to the rear of the building. The children who go there, come from all over Amsterdam's city centre. Tourists are sometimes totally shocked when they see the nursery school. Children next to window prostitution, they just can't grasp that. It's not as if these children play on the street in front of the windows or go inside, but if that was the case they would be the last ones to care. I know plenty of stories from people who really enjoyed running an errand now and then for the window prostitutes when they were children.

As to children who grow up in brothels in the Wallen – something that I have never yet come across myself – I find an interesting pamphlet in the municipal archives that is dated April 7, 1908. It gives a picture of how people thought back then: *"An Amsterdammer expresses his fury about the 'trade in women's flesh' in a brothel on the Oudezijds Achterburgwal near the Bethaniënstraat. The girls there entice clients to come in from behind the curtains and give them cold tea instead of cognac. Pimp Snip (nickname 'Kakkie') is the owner of the brothel. He has two children, nine and thirteen, with a hunchbacked servant girl, but he lives together with a Catholic woman. One of the children was seen sitting on the lap of one of the girls and that was enough reason to revoke Snip's parental rights. Because as they say: 'when the old folks sing, the young folks chirp'".*

Former community police officer, Joep de Groot, arrives wearing his iconic red wooden clogs and says: "Yes, in my time there were always families with children in the area, but not so many.

We don't really experience much trouble with youth in the neighbourhood. Some kids followed in the footsteps of their parents and got involved with drugs, but the majority of children that I've seen growing up here have done fine. The children who live here aren't dim-witted sheep. They see enough bad examples. My boys are almost in their fifties now, but they caught on to what went on here in the neighbourhood pretty quickly. I would take them out with me. We went for a cup of tea by someone on the Oudekerksplein and they were outside playing soccer. Then I would see how they kicked the ball closer and closer to the windows 'by accident'. They concluded that 'the women were too poor to buy clothing'. I explained to them that there were a lot of men who did not get enough attention and that they could get it from these women. There were also women who were 'blackmailed' by children. They would play just long enough in front of a window until they got some candy and a request to play with the ball a bit further away". Joep is full of stories. We arrange to meet shortly in the Koffieschenkerij cafe at the Oude Kerk to continue our chat.

"It is 1986. A young man is standing in front of my window with a hungry look in his eyes. When he comes in he says that he has never 'done it' before. I think that he is a little younger than me. I ask him why he doesn't want to wait until he can do it with a girl that he is in love with. I am a romantic at heart. Your first time should be out of love. But he doesn't want to wait to know what it's like. Now fine then. But first the money. Fifty guilders. There are plenty of young men passing by the windows, mostly in groups. As a challenge to each other they come and ask what it costs. I don't know if they are from the neighbourhood. It doesn't matter. I would have probably done the same and it is pretty funny. Sometimes I answer jokingly: 'Come on back when you know how it works'. This young man came on his own. Pretty brave. It's an honour to be someone's first. Then you will never be forgotten. I am aware of the responsibility and because of that I am not always in the mood. When the guy walks out the door twenty minutes or so later – I took it slow with him – he is more mature. When he gets home his mother will look at him with surprise and wonder what has changed about him. His father will get it right away".

Cafe the Zeevaart sits on the corner of the Korte Niezel and the Oudezijds Achterburgwal. At the beginning of the last century it was known as cafe 't Hoekje. It's a local bar where old guard residents also come for a beer. There are only a few of them still in the Wallen. Funny enough I have never been here for a drink before, so it's high time. Robin wants a beer and we soon fall into conversation with a couple of older men who keep an eye on the street from behind the window. "If you sit here for a few hours everyday, you'll know within a week exactly what's going on," one of them says. He was born shortly after the war and has lived in the Wallen since he was a young boy. His father was a milkman. When I ask him which time period was the best, he says that he finds the current time pretty good. "It was a mess before, although the city didn't do anything to help. That's how it goes," he says. "Every neighbourhood where they want to takeover the buildings, they first let everything fall into disrepair so that they can eventually snap it all up for nothing. Then they turn around and resell the buildings for a lot of money and afterwards fill their pockets with the leasehold". Someone else sitting at the table confirms that and then goes on to mention that he got a flu shot today. "But they couldn't get through his tough hide," says his son who has joined us. "He has worker arms. They are made of steel and no needle can get through".

Rob is the owner of the Zeevaart cafe. I ask him how he deals with drunk patrons. "If someone has really had enough to drink, I tell them," Rob says. "Then we just cut them off. If people come in already drunk, we send them away. That makes a big difference in earnings, but this is a small, quiet neighbourhood bar; we don't want anything to do with the screaming hordes. But of course they just go somewhere else. You have to have police presence in the Wallen to keep things under control. They are the only ones who can do something about the nuisance. The officers that are there are fantastic, but there aren't enough of them and the city regulators don't dare to do anything. I get that, you know. I also wouldn't run to try to take beer away from a group of drunk, strapping, English tourists.

These days it's mostly people from the provinces and tourists who come to the Wallen. Then they come and sit here on a terrace with their white wine and expensive handbags, to look at the women working behind the windows while convinced that they are all forced to do this work. I don't get that. I know one of the women who works next to here for years. She is married and has children. Her husband never comes here because then it's immediately assumed he's a pimp. People have no idea what they are talking about. They have an opinion about what other people do and tell you how you should live your life. That's so exhausting". Rob points to one of the men sitting at a table. "That's Toon. He's lived here his whole life, since 1936. And his father before him. But these days for every older resident who leaves, a yuppie or expat replaces them. Once in a while students, who live in an apartment rented for them by their father, will come in here. After a bit they start complaining how it's so rowdy on the street. Sure, then go live by the Amstel. This is an entertainment district. It's nonsense that they are now saying 'that the Wallen should be returned to the residents'. Mrs. Iping (former Amsterdam City Councillor) is saying that. She doesn't even live in the Wallen".

I look around at the people sitting here at the table by the window. All of them are residents. Authentic residents. Average age, seventy years old. They don't live in an expensive canal house elsewhere, no, they have lived here in the middle of the chaos of the Oudezijds Achterburgwal and the Oudekerksplein since they were children. Not that they don't complain about things. They definitely do that, and especially about trash. "Tourists are pretty conscientious you know," says Rob. "But the trash bins are either overflowing or there are too few and difficult to find. They removed the trash bin that was out front here, while I would have gladly changed the trash bag myself every day. Now the new bins are placed further away from the bridge and that means the pizza box just gets tossed on the ground". After a last round they let us leave with the promise that we'll come back some time. We are all too happy to do that.

When we are back on the street, we take a moment to reflect while standing on the bridge over the Oudezijds Achterburgwal. Behind me is the Mata Hari restaurant, named after a notorious casino that used to be there. When I turn to tell Robin about it, I see that she is chatting with someone a little further on. She was taking photos by a sex cinema and one of the cashiers was giving her a talking to. Robin showed him the photos she had taken and promised to send him a copy. He appreciated that. At the same time he takes the opportunity to ask her out to dinner. I had to laugh. It reminds me of the time we were in San Francisco together. Naturally we ended up in a rundown area. The streets were strewn with tents, junk and interesting people. Just when I wasn't looking Robin had crossed the street and stood photographing a wall mural featuring Michael Jackson. There came a large, fierce-looking man running towards her. I rushed across but that ended up being totally unnecessary. Just like her, he was also a fan of Jackson and they were having a great time chatting with each other. I love seeing how non-judgemental and relaxed Robin is, how she doesn't scare easily and just does her own thing.

> "It is 1986. 'What's a nice girl like you doing in this business?' asks a client as he dresses himself while I straighten the large bath towel on the bed. I am irritated by his hypocritical question but don't comment on it. If this is the kind of question he can come up with, then there is no way he will get the answer. He ties the laces of his fancy shoes, stands up, and symbolically brushes non-existent dirt from his trousers. I am getting angry and quickly turn towards the washbasin. I wash his sweat from my body with soap and water and put my work outfit on again: a black and silver body stocking that an old lady from the neighbourhood

crocheted for me. Maybe I could ask him what business he has here if he thinks it's so bad? No, I don't have the energy for that. Actually, I have zero interest in discussions about my work. More often I get clients who think they need to rescue me or something. They're even worse than the people out on the street who think we're all working here against our will. What do I need to be rescued from and what are you doing here if you think it's so awful? Let me be. I do what I do and don't ask me why. At least Lennaert Nijgh understood that."

Politics today

"I think that there are a number of things going on at the same time in the Wallen," says Mayor Femke Halsema, while she and Robin clean out the candy dish together. We spoke earlier with her in her office at city hall and meet again now in cafe 't Mandje on the Zeedijk. "The majority of the window prostitutes are migrants and in many cases I don't know how they came here and if they are really completely autonomous. That concerns me. Another thing, and it's not something the women can do anything about themselves, is that the Wallen has become an international tourist attraction, to a degree that we often don't like. That also leads to the unwelcome degradation of the women standing behind the windows. Too often I see window prostitutes being laughed at and photographed. Then you might argue that this is 'a question of enforcement', but sometimes it's impossible to control this kind of thing. And another problem are the links with criminality".

The current debate about the future of the Wallen seems like a continuation of the discussion over the last thirteen years, though with a different approach. After the fiasco of Project 1012 however, not everyone in the Wallen trusts plans coming from the city council. In particular, the proposed scenario that involves relocating the window brothels and maybe even the entire erotic sector is causing a lot of alarm.

"Fears about the past are preventing people from really listening to what I am saying," Halsema continues. "I think that more sex workers need to be able to do their work openly and legally, but there is nothing that says that the Wallen is the only and best place for this. I think that we have to look very closely at whether we can both strengthen the rights of the women and ensure that nuisance is reduced for residents and others in the neighbourhood. The question is if you can kill two birds with one stone. Either way window prostitution in the Wallen is a shrinking sector, whether we intervene now or not. That's in part due to past interventions by the city, but also because of the internet and other developments. I have always said that there are three objectives when it comes to the Wallen. As far as I am concerned everything beyond that is totally open to discussion as long as these objectives are achieved: strengthening women's rights, reducing the level of nuisance, and severing links to crime. These objectives are more important to me than the scenarios, by which I really want to stimulate discussion. From all the previous discussions we know that if the the municipality pushes the Wallen, it will only be met with resistance and that won't get us anywhere. I want city council to think about what they want, together with residents and business owners".

Mayor Femke Halsema's mission is clear in its objectives, but she also has to deal with the rest of city council. "I'm not making any moral judgement here," the Mayor continues. "My strongest personal memory of the Wallen is from when I was a criminology student and I interviewed clients for a research project on prostitution. They had a private chat group then called KLEP. I was in my early twenties then and went to a group meeting with a friend. My friend was an attractive woman with blond hair. One man in the group tried to sweet-talk her into trying prostitution. 'She would be able to make good money,' he said. Sitting next to her I didn't know if I should be insulted or shocked.

You see, my perspective when it comes to sex work is pretty pragmatic. It's a market with supply and demand. But the workers always have be able to work freely and with dignity. I don't want any exploitation and contempt for women in the Wallen. And I also don't want them to be ridiculed. If people were to ask me if I would like it if one of my daughters went to work in prostitution, like they often ask you, I would definitely say no, preferable not. I would add that my children have the freedom to make their own choices. Should they choose to anyway then I would respect that, although begrudgingly. In the same way that I would begrudgingly respect their choice to join the military.

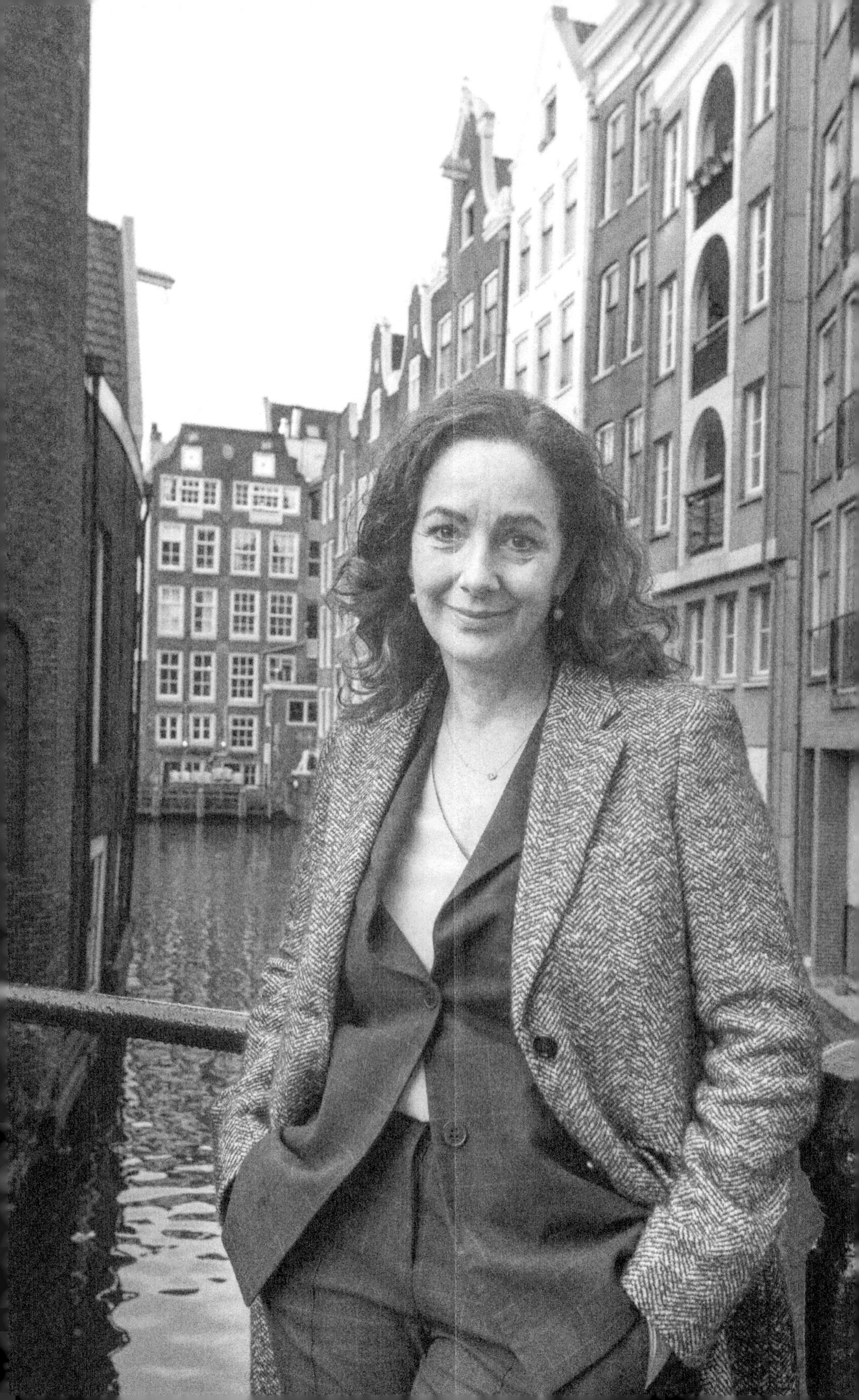

The emotional and physical risks of military service are often too much and I have other hopes for my children".

I am curious about Halsema's opinion about Project 1012. How did she look at it as a resident of Amsterdam and does she want to take a different approach? "At the time that Project 1012 was happening I didn't follow it closely," the Mayor answers. "I did learn from the project. It was framed too negatively from the beginning and it had far too little perspective on how the city centre should evolve, for example. The problem of large tourist groups visiting an area that is becoming smaller was partly created by reducing the number of windows. But I do understand the attempt to alter the character of at least a part of the old historic centre by doing so.

I have a different objective and tone. There really has been a shift in the discussion. I notice that there is a greater willingness within city council to collaborate. I think it's nonsense that the Wallen won't be the same without window brothels. It will always be a unique area. I find it really problematic that it's uniqueness at the moment is thanks to prostitution and coffee shops. It is one of the most beautiful city centres in Europe. I don't want it to be completely 'swept clean' and that the last sex worker leaves the neighbourhood. That is totally not what I am striving for. The Wallen is an old working-class neighbourhood and it's okay that there is a bit of disorder. But I want the centre to fit what we want it to be as Amsterdam and not that the city's image is shaped by sex and drugs – that we get hordes of drunken tourists who eat at Kentucky Fried Chicken, visit the Wallen, sleep in the car and then leave again.

In order for the Wallen to survive in the long term, we have to change something. There is no timeline and nothing is set in stone. We are taking a cautious new step which is exploring the possibility of a prostitution hotel – actually I find that an ugly word – and exploring whether relocating the windows is possible. With Project 1012 everything happened too top-down and was very heavy-handed. We are not doing it that way anymore.

Say that you decide that the number of windows in the Wallen needs to be reduced, then that costs a lot of money. If that's what you want then where do we get the money from? My long-term vision is that the centre will become a low-traffic and very liveable part of our city where, next to the sex workers, there are also workspaces, where young artists from the south-east of the city can find a studio and where Amsterdammers from other parts of the city are happy to visit again. Change always makes people nervous and I get it that there is distrust in the neighbourhood after everything that has happened. I am not in any rush. Besides, if I initiate one change that results in less nuisance in the neighbourhood, but which negatively impacts the human rights of sex workers, then I would consider that to be a totally failed project. So we are going to think very carefully about this".

A few weeks after our discussion the mayor announced plans to develop a sex hotel or erotic centre outside of the Wallen. This summer the city council will decide if they support the plan.

We had arrived at café 't Mandje from off the bridge by the Zeevaart and turning left on the Zeedijk. Now we are heading in the other direction on 'the dijk' to the Chinese area. In our opinion, if you want to eat Chinese then this is the place to be, unless you are willing to settle for less. The Zeedijk is often called the border of the Wallen. However, if you dive into the history and development of the area it's clear that both the Zeedijk and the Geldersekade – where a few window brothels can still be found and where a lot of hustling once happened – were a part of the old city. In the sixties there were also a couple of window brothels on the Zeedijk. Pubs and inns where 'women of easy virtue' and their customers met, established quickly once the Zeedijk was constructed. According to the oldest written records, Amsterdam's first inn was established around 1350. The one on the Zeedijk had a reputation of being of a 'dubious quality: they provided opportunity to prostitutes, and the patrons gambled, drank, cursed and fought'. When you walk through the street now, it's hard to imagine.

"When the Buddhist temple was completed your grandfather painted it," I announce with pride as we stand in front admiring it. Across from the temple is the Chinese restaurant Nam Kee. It was our regular place to eat for a long time, until we moved next-door to the New King. Robin has come here since she was a child and still eats here regularly together with her father.

STORMSTEEG
Centrum
順風里
CAFÉ-SLIJTERIJ
„Oost-West"
ANNO 1731
TEL-249770
LLE BEKENDE MERKEN GEDISTILLEERD
ALHIER VERKRIJGBAAR!
2

"It is 1986. I start work at eight and on work nights we usually eat beforehand at Nam Kee. As always I order lean barbecue pork (Cha Siu) with extra sauce and vegetables. Tonight I'll give Old Daan – 'move along!' he always yelled at everyone on the street – a five guilder tip to get me another portion if I get hungry. Then I'll eat it from a plastic container with a plastic spoon while sitting on my barstool behind the window and the whole room will smell like the sauce. Anyway, that's no worse than the haze from my cigarette smoke. No one has ever complained about it. At Nam Kee my tablemates are friends. Also a little bit my 'babysitters' and one of them is my lover. I learn to eat rice the Asian way with a spoon and fork or from a bowl with chopsticks. Lots of sambal but not the really hot kind. The guys slurp up their soup with gusto. It has the same meat in it that I feed Santa. Yuck. One of the guys speaks a little Chinese and that, along with the fact that we eat here almost everyday and are clearly from the neighbourhood, means that we always get a table in this busy restaurant. At least, that's how I imagine it. After eating we leave and walk through the Molensteeg towards the canal. I turn left to head to my window and the guys walk to Alessandro, their regular hangout, to do their own thing. The day can begin".

The Molensteeg didn't have the best reputation. It seemed that something was always going on there. We knew the workrooms to be bad there and that's saying something. My first workroom had quite a few cockroaches as 'regular clients', so I was used to a lot. Around the late-nineties there were rumours that the women in the Molensteeg were forced to work behind the window. There were a couple of scary Turkish and Yugoslavian pimps around the Wallen and some of the East-European sex workers came accompanied by burly criminal types. Based on the stories we heard later, certain pimps had developed some brutal methods to ensure a small group of women kept working. It seems strange that this could have happened in such a busy neighbourhood where so many people, police and support organisations are involved with such issues. It shows how the whole thing is not that simple. I abhor the idea of forced (sex)work and know for certain that most people in the Wallen feel the same. Since the lifting of the ban on brothels in 2000, regulation and attention to working conditions has improved the situation. There is also a lot that has improved from within the industry thanks to conscientious brothel owners, sex worker organisations and health institutions. The problems are not completely eradicated, but because they are too interwoven with global issues, you cannot simply solve things through stricter regulations in the Wallen. Regardless, Project 1012 went on as if trafficking was happening on a large scale in the Wallen. The topic catches the imagination. Everyone finds it really awful and wants to do something about it. As a politician you need public opinion to be on your side and it's possible to achieve a lot by talking about trafficking. Then no one will ask you, for example, why you used millions of public funds to buy out a window brothel owner in order to change the character of the neighbourhood. I'm going to be bold and suggest that the topic of trafficking has explicitly been used to advance the gentrification process of the Wallen over the last thirteen years. But how do you talk about the misuse and statistical manipulation of the issue, without doing a disservice to the fact that it is happening?

Trafficking, what's the deal?

Heleen Driessen is the prostitution confidant at the sex worker support and health centre (P&G292) in Amsterdam. The first time that I met her was when I was visiting the mobile unit at the (closed) streetwalking zone on the Theemsweg. "Everything that's not going well in the industry comes to me," she says. "It can be about bad working conditions in a brothel, complaints concerning inspections by city officials and situations such as forced prostitution. Most sex workers, about four thousand per year, come to us, but I also take a weekly walk along the windows. Sometimes a brothel owner will call and ask me to come by because they have concerns about someone.

Most trafficking happens in the unlicensed sector and also to some degree in the Wallen," Helen says. "Sometimes it's clearly exploitation. But anyway, that's something that we can never completely rule out. It's also not easy to recognise. I have had cases where someone is a victim that I would never have expected. As part of my role with Amsterdam's Coordination Centre for Human Trafficking I have travelled to countries where people are being taught to work as beggars or in prostitution. It makes sense that they go to places such as the Netherlands or another European country where they can earn money and work in safety. People often think we can't talk about freedom of choice if someone opts to do this work because of debt or poverty. That still doesn't mean it's a situation of trafficking.

I think what is important with an area where sex work is concentrated, like in the Wallen, is that sex workers have always indicated that they feel safe there. And that we can always drop in. Traffickers operate in underground locations because they are out of sight and we have no access. A victim will never just walk up and ask for help. Trust has to be established and you need to be able to find each other easily".

"The stereotypical image of trafficking is of 'innocent' girls and women forced into prostitution against their will. However, this is relatively rare", says Marjan Wijers, trafficking expert and current PhD research candidate in sex work and human rights at the University of Essex in England. "If you look at trafficking cases in the Netherlands, the majority are not about being forced into prostitution, but force and exploitation in prostitution: people who consciously choose to work in prostitution, but then find themselves in situations of exploitation where, for example, they are forced to work under conditions they do not choose or are pressured to hand over their earnings to someone else".

Everyone has a different understanding of trafficking. In criminal law, trafficking involves force, violence and deception with the goal of exploiting someone. There is always a third party or several people involved. You see how the debate is being muddied by so many people who are saying: 'Yes, but economic force is force too'. But if you say everyone who is not rich enough to survive without working is forced, then it becomes quite complicated. Another factor corrupting the debate is the possible underlying moral judgement. The idea that no one can work voluntarily in prostitution. If you believe this then you quickly come to the conclusion that all prostitution is forced. That's why statistics vary so much.

An important question is: where does the border lie between bad working conditions that should be addressed through labour rights, and situations that are so bad or restrictive so as to constitute a violation of human rights requiring the use of criminal law. Historically labour rights are the most important and successful instrument we have to protect people from exploitation and abuse of power in a labour situation. But if you use violence to force someone to work in prostitution or deny them the right to refuse clients or services, to have autonomy over their body and life, then you are committing a crime.

If you look a research statistics – including research commissioned by the government – then the number of sex workers in the Netherlands who experience or have experienced force lies somewhere between 4 and 10%. This research also shows that the majority of women are able to get out of the situation themselves. Without police intervention. Per year we are talking about an average of around one hundred to one hundred and fifty cases of human trafficking in the Netherlands nationally. There is no statistical basis to the idea that there is a lot of trafficking in the Wallen. Statistics gathered by the National Rapporteur for Human Trafficking showed only two cases of suspected victims of trafficking in Amsterdam's window brothels in the period from 2011 to 2015".

> "It is 2017. Robin and I are with a friend in Bucharest. One evening we speak with two women who are working on the street. They would both like to go to western-Europe to earn money for their families. It doesn't matter what kind of work. Only that's just not possible for them. They look very different from the Romanian women working in the Wallen. No smoothly styled hair, ultra-toned figure or trendy clothes. They don't say it but I suspect that they are Roma. Poor, with a darker skin tone and uneducated. One of them can neither read nor write and has five young children. She would prefer to not work in prostitution, but doesn't see any other options. She is one of many. What she really wants is an education and a job, but she won't get either. Then it's sex work, she can survive with that. You get used to everything. She does find it hard that because of her work she's landed even lower on the social ladder. She hates it that people look down on her while she is doing the same as they are, just working to feed her children. You do what you can using what's available to you".

"That was a new situation for me," Robin says. "Being confronted by the poverty and stories during our visit to Romania. I had never experienced something like that. Of course it's not that all the Romanian women who work here in the sex industry come from poor families, but that is what we encountered during our travels. I found it interesting to hear these women's stories, the dilemmas they face and the choices that they make. Just to survive they do something different from what they would really like to be doing. It makes me feel helpless seeing that there is little chance of improvement and that they can't do anything about it. Everyone has had moments where you have to give something up for the bigger picture. To me that's strength. These women work for their own lives and that of their children. I respect that".

We backtrack a bit along the Zeedijk until we are at the Boomsteeg. From this viewpoint you clearly see that the Zeedijk sits higher than the area we are looking out towards. It's strange to think about where we are standing. A very long time in the past the waves of the Zuiderzee pounded against the protective sea walls here behind us. I imagine enormous sailing ships with cannons, mooring in the harbour around the corner and rolling kegs of beer down the gangplanks directly into the beer cellars of dubious inns and pubs in the neighbourhood.

Some of the window brothels in the Boomsteeg sit a couple of steps below street level. They were perfect hidey-holes for drug users if no one was working. Dark and out of sight. You can still sit there. The windows in the Boomsteeg were owned by Charrel Geerts in the nineties. Put under pressure by Project 1012, he sold his buildings to the city for around twenty-five million euro. They were allowed to stand empty for a number of years after that. Since 2017 the windows are being run by My Red Light, a non-profit organisation prioritising the well-being of sex workers, and where the people renting from them have participatory rights.

The previous mayor, Mayor van der Laan, was the driving force behind this – in principle wonderful – project. It became known as the 'municipal brothel' and caused a lot of neighbourhood discussion for how it was presented. Probably the biggest error committed was the Mayor's comment that sex workers 'would have the possibility to work here pimp-free'. Naturally, to the outside world that sounded fantastic, but I thought that Van der Laan's comment put everyone on the wrong track. However well-meaning his statement was, things aren't that simple. As the passing of time has shown us, it is possible for someone with a pimp to rent a window from My Red Light. And just as with other brothel owners, the moment you find out that it's going on you can try to make a coordinated effort do something about it.

Jade works in the Boomsteeg. In her workroom, located one floor above the window where she stands, she talks about how she deals with work, the tourists in the neighbourhood and what she thinks about the city's possible plans for the window brothels in the Wallen.

"I came to Amsterdam as a student," explains Jade. "I decided to work next to my studies and chose sex work. I had no experience yet. My studies were also related to sex work, but sex work as work, instead of a form of trafficking. I wanted to compare the Netherlands and where I came from, because there are big policy differences. That the work is legal here in the Netherlands was interesting to me and I wanted to look more closely at that. I have been working for three and a half years now. Sex work suits me. I was surprised to see just how immediately comfortable it felt to me. I have good social skills and like to please people. I have absolutely no problem if people have so-called strange preferences or a unique body odour. It's actually nice that everyone is so different. What I did underestimate, is just how difficult it is to live with a secret. The stigma that a lot of sex workers suffer from, had a greater impact on me than I could have imagined before starting. It is really difficult to have to lie to my family. In particular as it's a topic about which I also argue it shouldn't be necessary to lie about.

I enthusiastically told my housemates when I started working. One said that they had difficulty with the idea that I would be having sex with different men for money. I said that it wasn't a problem at all with me and asked my housemate why he did have trouble with it. For the first time I realised that I couldn't just tell everyone and maybe even needed to be careful if I wanted other work or to study further in the future. I stopped for a year because living a double life had taken its toll. I went to work as a waitress in a restaurant which was awful. The only positive thing about that job was that if someone asked what I did for work I could give an honest answer.

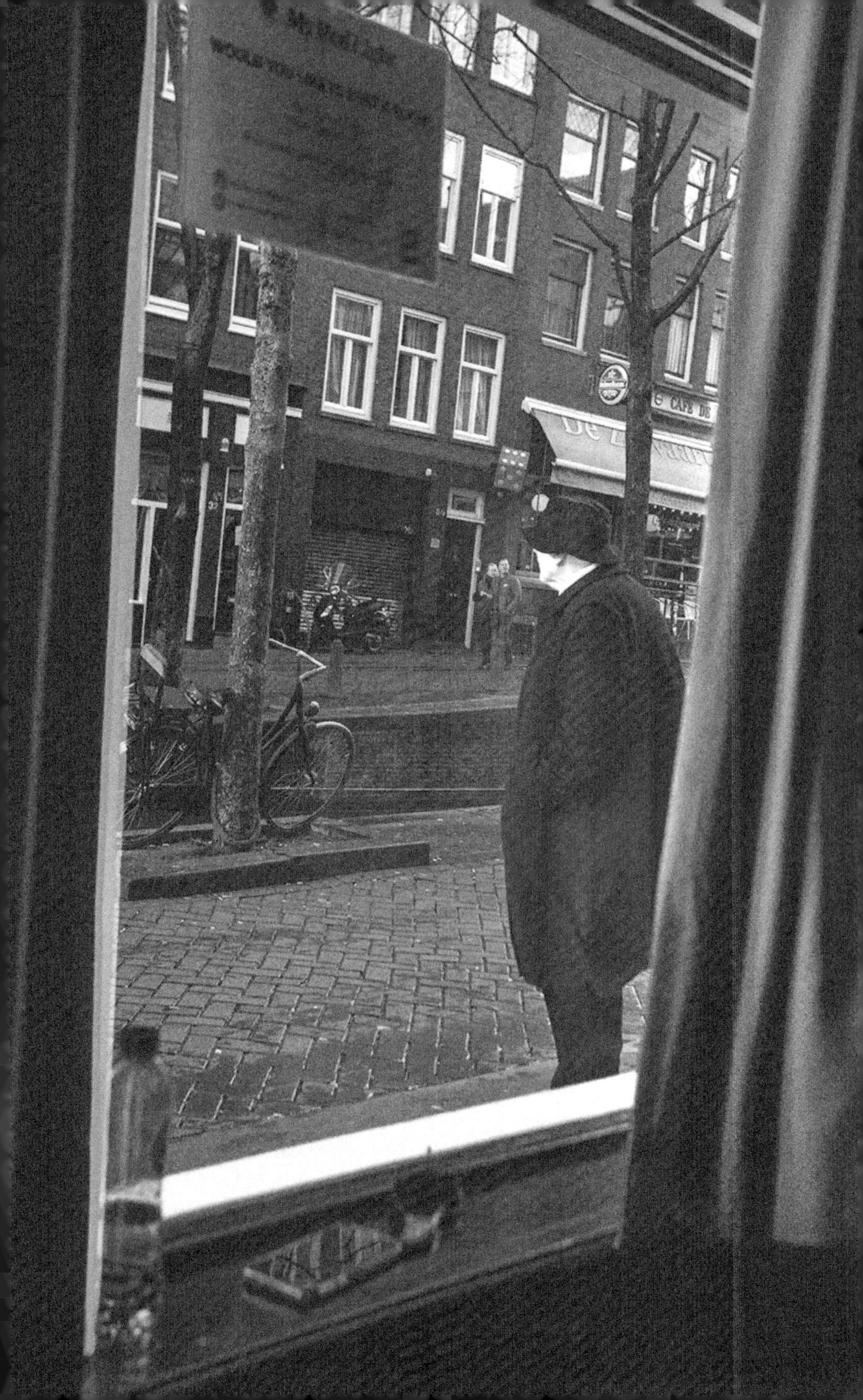
CAFE DE

Patrons at the restaurant could be really rude, but I had to serve them with a smile just the same to avoid getting into trouble with my boss. As a sex worker I am my own boss. Especially in this setting. Of course it's annoying when people walking past my window are rude, but if I want to I can say something back, draw the curtain to shut them out and I can refuse clients who are rude.

Before coming back to the Wallen, I worked in a private brothel for a time. It was fun, but the earnings were really low. Clients pay sixty-five euro for a half hour and after all the taxes my take was only twenty. In the meantime I started working behind the window again. As soon as I was back I noticed that a few things had changed in the neighbourhood in that year. There were more tourist groups walking around and more photographs were being taken of us than in the past. It seems really much quieter the last few months. Just the same, people stop and just stand in front of my window staring at me. It's made me think about whether I want to keep doing this. I just get so tired of it sometimes.

You can tell by people's faces what they think about you. Some faces just ooze disgust and the comments that you can hear from behind the window are sometimes really hurtful. Especially when they come from women, and that's most of the time. They feel they are better than us and they want everyone to know it. I quickly turn up the music when I hear that. I'm lucky that I have friends who know what I do and are okay with it. I also get a lot of support from my colleagues. That's why I know that how people react to what I do for work is no reflection on who I am. It just shows what they are made of. Sometimes I have to remind myself of this. Despite all these people's behaviour, I stand straight and proud behind my window and I still laugh. The Mayor says that we are being degraded, but actually the people on the street are degrading themselves".

Sitting on the window seat in Jade's workroom I look outside. I know how it feels to be looked at in that way and would like it if the people on the street realised this.

"I don't have a problem being on display and looked at," Jade continues. "I don't care if hundreds of people walk by. It also doesn't interest me if someone doesn't like what I do.

But people shouldn't be rude. I am a big supporter of information and education. And then not through sensationalism because that also doesn't help us. There are a lot of people who come to the Wallen with no understanding of sex work and who feel uncertain about prostitution. It's important to give the right information because then they walk through the neighbourhood in another way and see us differently. I generally don't have anything against tours either, as long as they don't park themselves in front of my window or take photos. Sometimes I see the local hosts from the city talking to people who are taking pictures, and that does help. I think that the city needs to put more effort into telling people that sex work is work. They don't have to paint a rosy picture, it's enough if they just say that it is what it is".

I ask Jade why she chose to work at this location. "I work with My Red Light because I feel good here," she answers. "Some of the people here in the office have also done this work. They understand how it is and that makes me feel more respected as a person rather than just a renter who they make money from. I have debated working on the Ruysdaelkade or in the Singel area, but because more Dutch clients go there and fewer tourists, I opted for the Wallen. I am most comfortable working with tourists. There are also other benefits to working in the Wallen: you can go and join in with the masses out on the street without it being immediately obvious that you are a sex worker. In an exclusive area with only windows that would be different. If the city closes the windows in the Wallen that would break me. This is how I want to work. I don't fit in a club or a high-class escort agency. I don't want to work from home because I don't want clients in my house. I could go back to a private brothel, but I don't look forward to the low payouts. If the windows are going to be moved, I wonder where. I can't just up and move with them, especially if that's outside of the city and far from everyday life. I feel safe here because it's also a residential area. Moreover, it's fun in the Wallen.

My Red Light is going to pilot a new initiative: 'working behind closed curtains'. The idea is that you find your clients online instead of standing behind the window. It's not for me. I want to be able to look a client in the eye before deciding to let him inside and I don't want my photo on the internet. But there are also colleagues who think it might be great because then they don't have to deal with all the gawkers. It's good if there's a choice. After all, sex workers are also a really diverse group of people".

Jade goes to get ready for work and we say our goodbyes. From the Boomsteeg we turn left and head up the canal. There are quite a lot of people walking around and now and then a large tourist group. I see Asians and a striking number of Spanish speaking people. There are couples of all ages, groups of boys having a laugh and once in a while a man walking alone. He is looking for something; walking around in his own little world. I recognise the clients. One man is aware of where he is and a little uncertain. He thinks people are looking at him. He's new at this. The other has experience and isn't bothered by the people around him. He believes he is unobserved or anonymous. He's focussed and enjoying the game. He walks up and down the canals making a few rounds before he chooses.

> "It is 1987. I'm standing in the Oudekennissteeg and I am not sure yet if I enjoy working here more. On the canal there's more distance between you and people, and I can scan easier for clients. Then I can size them up better. In the alleyway they walk so close by that I have less time to decide if I am interested in him or not. It's probably the same for them I assume. What do they actually think about? I pay attention to how they are dressed and their appearance. They must do that too. The most important difference is that I think about the money while they think about the sex. I can easily pick out a client. I only need to look into their eyes. If someone I see walks by the third time looking at me, then I know there is a big chance that he'll end up coming in. He just needs to recharge or gather up the courage. Or he doesn't want the enjoyment to be over too soon. Usually cumming means it's time to go back home while wandering around allows time to fantasise over what's about to happen. I get it. But in reality I couldn't care less. I forget most of them the minute they walk out the door".

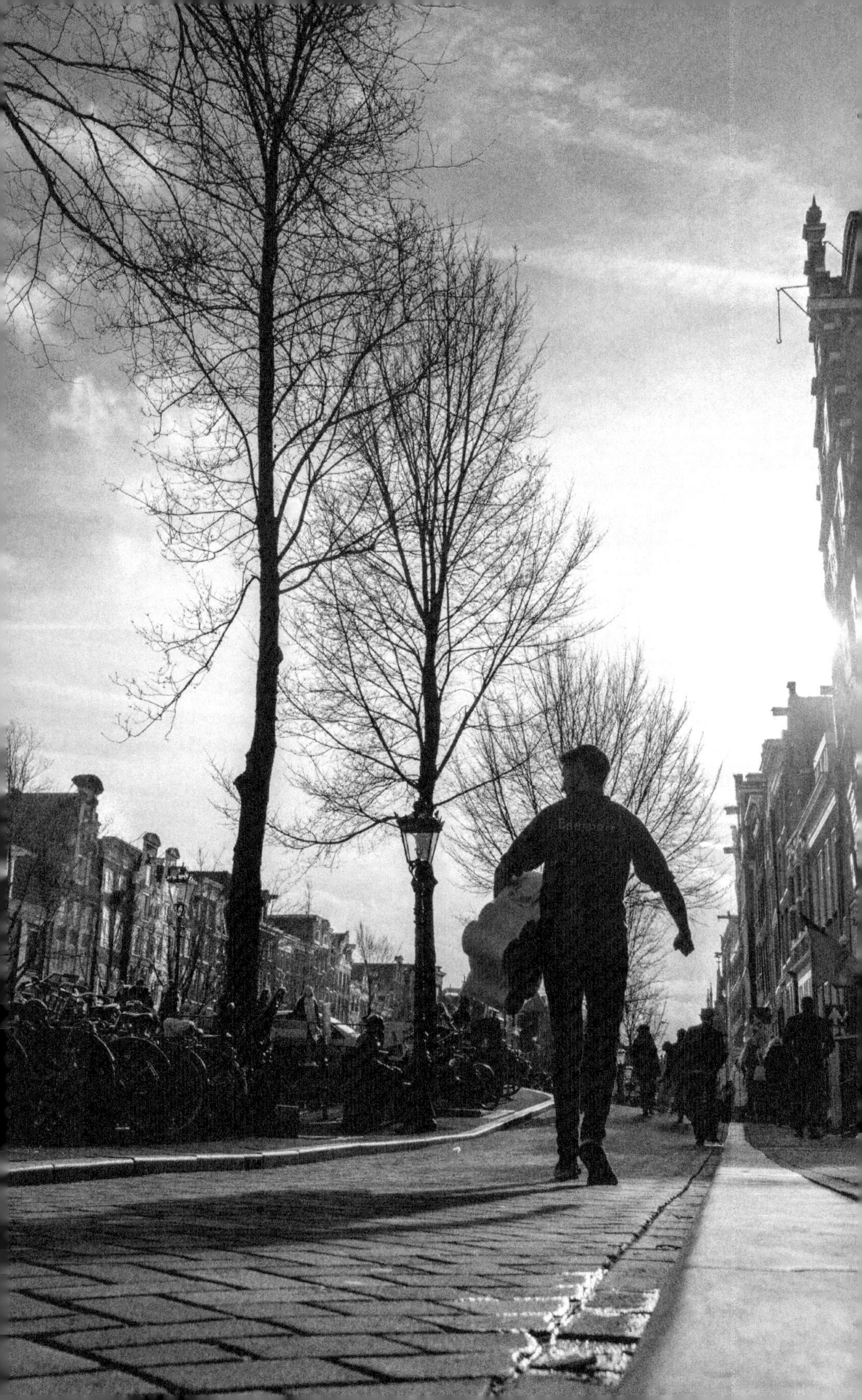

It is quiet on the canal and the atmosphere is good. A lot of the windows are unoccupied with a 'room to rent' sign hanging. It's later in the afternoon. The evening shift doesn't start until after seven o'clock. In the evening there are more people on the street, but the relative quiet during the day and a different type of client is what some sex workers prefer. It's personal. I never did well during the day. I think that I didn't make a good impression in the daylight.

Before women from East-Europe came to work in the Wallen, this section of the canal was where African and South American women stood. Once in a while a Dutch or German woman with an addiction sat there and often also older women. It didn't always go well for everyone. This was at a time when – except for the Salvation Army and the nuns – there weren't any organisations that could offer help and it was before health services appointed a prostitution confidant for sex workers. Together with the Oudekerksplein and the Molensteeg, this 'half' of the Wallen charged less rent for workrooms and the women's fees were proportionally lower. The other side of what is now known as the Major Bosshardt bridge and the Oudekennissteeg, was the so-called better half. There you found mainly Dutch and Asian women, just as in the Sint Annenkwartier a little further up. In a later period you could find transgender sex workers working in a small side street off of the canal.

Towards the year 2000 a lot had changed in the neighbourhood. When the borders opened, more and more women came from East-Europe. The laws changed for prostitution and allowed only those coming from a European Union country or in possession of a work permit to work legally. The majority of African and Thai workers disappeared. The group from South America stayed pretty much the same. A few of them found creative solutions to be able to work legally in the Wallen. They either managed to get a Dutch passport through Curaçao or married someone, often a regular client, who was Dutch.

It wasn't only buildings and streets that were being improved, but also more and more window brothels. In expectation that the national government would lift the ban on brothels in 2000, the municipality of Amsterdam started to introduce new rules for brothels already around 1997. Window brothels had to be of a certain size and satisfy hygiene requirements in order to improve sex worker's working conditions.

The upholstered wall coverings were replaced with tiles, and curtains, beds and the barstools were upgraded. Within some buildings a number of larger rooms were divided into several smaller spaces. The busy street traffic was also addressed. Now it's no longer permitted to drive along the canal in the evenings and at nighttime and the number of parking spaces have been greatly reduced. With no parking things are much quieter on the Oudezijds Achterburgwal and it looks lovely, but for sex workers there is one big disadvantage: tourists sit picnicking along the canal in the summer and are constantly watching and photographing the sex workers behind the windows.

We walk past the Banana Bar and arrive at the Major Bosshardt bridge. If you turn on your axis here, you have enough material to write a book. The Old Sailor cafe where it's always a nuthouse on nights when there is a soccer match, the black building where the Banana Bar is and which was once home to the Church of Satan, the abbeys that once stood in the Monnikenstraat and the Bloedstraat a little further up.

Close to the Salvation Army chapel, at the corner of the Molensteeg, there is a window brothel now, but 'in my time' this is where the Yüksel snack bar stood. There is also a window brothel on the other side of the canal, on the other corner, where the Alessandro Lunchroom used to be. We bought condoms and paper towels there. You can buy paper towels in almost every store in the Wallen, sometimes for ridiculously high prices. It's used mostly to remove condoms because no self-respecting prostitute would ever do that with bare hands of course. The pimps and boyfriends hung around on the corner by Alessandro's and kept a close eye on everything. If an alarm went off somewhere, they would storm off towards it. If people on the street were being annoying, they took care of it. And they also occasionally cleared the street of drug dealers. There was rarely an evening without a brawl.

Robin gets into a conversation with a man who thinks she is a tourist because of her camera. When she tells him what she is doing, he poses for her and tells a bit about himself. His name is Evert and he is Jewish. In one hand he has a hand-rolled cigarette and in the other a beer; secretly he's flirting a little with her. Evert says that he used to have an addiction, but only uses now if he has some extra money.

At the moment he is sleeping at the Salvation Army shelter. While he is telling us all this someone walks up toward him and cries out: 'What, I thought you were dead!' Robin uses the opportunity to walk away. I am also chatting with someone on the bridge. 'It's like a small village here,' we both say. You stop for one minute and within no time you're having a conversation with an acquaintance and someone else always comes by to chat for a bit. Evert calls out to Robin and tells her 'that she really needs to try a Jewish man once'. When someone she knows gives her a hug, he yells: 'Hey, don't touch my girl!' We all have a good laugh about it.

From the bridge I point out my first window to Robin, number 51. It looks a lot different than it was then. The window is also a door now. When I worked there the window had small panes and I sat between two wooden sash bars. My workroom was in the little hall. To the left there's a building with a cellar window and a window higher up. Once I was allowed to work in the upper window when the person who always rented it went on vacation.

"It is 1986. I am wearing white lingerie for the first time. A pretty bra and thong set. They really glow under the black light. My hair is wild and my eyes are black. I know that it's a beautiful image seen from the street. I have always wanted to stand in this window. It's big and sits high above the street. It feels like I am posing in a painting that hangs in a museum. Everyone earns good money here so it might not only be because of me that it's busy, but I don't care. Tonight is my night. People stare up at me as if they are looking at a futuristic piece of art. I am loving it. Outside it's dark, so the red light and the black light are really effective. I look seductively at male passers-by who I want as clients. I am in a good flow and almost constantly occupied. When I have earned a thousand guilders I wave to my boyfriend who is standing at the corner, press my legs together and make a painful face. He makes a circling motion with his hand meaning: keep going. I stick my tongue out at him and open a new tube of lubricant. Naughtily and insistent I wink at the first man who looks at me. He climbs meekly up the stairs and the curtains close once more".

Jan Broers is the owner of the building with the upper window. We meet with him and his wife Monique in the kitchen located behind the cellar window. When we were done working, we regularly went to have a drink with them in the Royal Taste hotel, which they also owned. It was the only hotel in the neighbourhood and the bar was still open at five in the morning, something that was still possible then. Jan's grandmother and aunt were also brothel owners.

Jan was born just before the war and he grew up in the Wallen. As a kid he would run errands for the – then still – Dutch window prostitutes on the Oudekerksplein, "in the time when people were still working for a knaak (rijksdaalder)". He knows the neighbourhood like no other. For Jan it's his home so it's not surprising that he reacts so strongly when the conversation turns to the future of the neighbourhood. You are not only messing with his business but also his roots. You touch his soul when you talk about the Wallen. If someone says that the neighbourhood is a criminal breeding ground, Jan feels personally attacked.

Monique came into his life when he had already bought his first building in the neighbourhood. In the meantime, they have been together for almost forty years and side by side they struggle for the survival of their business and the preservation of the Wallen. As Monique slices the apple pie and we are still pulling up our chairs, Jan kicks off: "do you still remember all the things Lodewijk Asscher said when he began with Project 1012? How he said that we were all criminals and the neighbourhood was the cesspool of the city? From that moment on it became even more difficult for us than it had been, for example, to keep our mortgages. Everyone looked at us with suspicion. You were constantly having to defend yourself. That wasn't totally new of course. We have always been looked down on, but because of Asscher it became worse".

I have several questions for Jan, but I know that he will keep coming back to his frustration over how things are currently going and Project 1012. I decide to just let him tell his story.

"I had my first brothel in the seventies", he says. "Before then I worked at the Waterlooplein market, but I met a woman who worked here on the corner of the canal and was able to buy a building for twenty-five thousand guilders. That's how I got started. In 1980 I bought the hotel and met Monique by Waterlooplein. Over the years I picked up a few more buildings. By the way, already then the bank wouldn't give us a mortgage. I had to make an agreement with the previous owner and pay him off every month. That's how we did it then. Then there were more possibilities than now". Monique adds: "The media plays a big role in how people think these days. When you keep writing about how bad it is in this neighbourhood, people believe that".

"I live for my business," Jan says. "I am always working on it. I was the first to expand the number of windows and to tile the workrooms. Do you still remember how the walls were all upholstered? Tiles were much more hygienic, I thought." Jan is indeed always busy fixing things somewhere, and is known for rarely wearing anything other than work clothes.

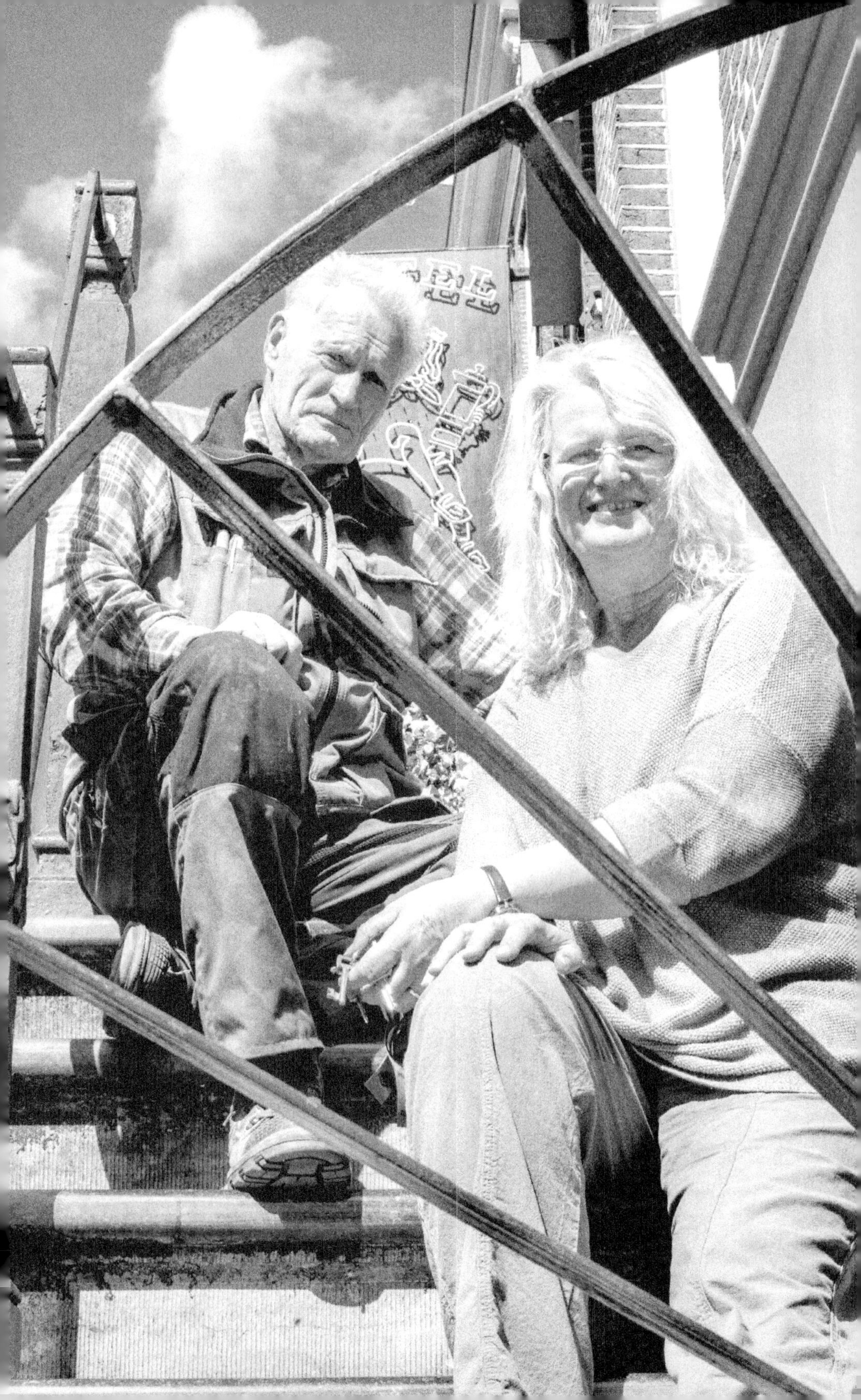

Monique doesn't want to leave the neighbourhood, but she would like to get out of the brothel business. "It's a handful," she says. "She's right," says Jan. "Our work hasn't gotten any easier with all the regulations and fighting with the government. There are women who have rented the same window from us for ten years and still they have to cough up the same story when a city official or other inspector comes along. That makes me angry so I send them packing. I tell them: 'Get lost, I run a clean ship; nothing nasty'. Being angry all the time is taking its toll on my body. Monique organises everything with the women and she hears their stories about how they are treated by the government. It's infuriating. And that while I am actually happy with regulations. In comparison to how it was, a lot has improved for the women".

"In the past a lot of them had to pay rent even on their days off if they wanted to keep their regular window and couldn't or almost never went on vacation because of that," Monique adds. "It's much better that they aren't allowed to work double shifts and around the clock anymore". "I have always found that was ridiculous," Jan says. "We've always done things in our own way when it comes to renting workrooms. I don't care for all that hassle. I have the advantage that these are my buildings so I can do that. Many brothel owners these days rent the space, so they need to earn a lot more money to cover the costs. Well anyway, Asscher has messed up so much in the neighbourhood. He was going to clean it all up. 'He was ashamed to walk around here' and that 'every day six hundred commercial rapes happened here,' remember that? Everything was about trafficking and that's how the people walking around the neighbourhood now see it. What he began in 2007, is still having an impact.

Everything was different before. Not necessarily better but it was just the way it was. It's pretty understandable that you sometimes long for the past, like you said. You were your own boss. Every cent you earned went into your own pocket. Never mind the tax department. Your man stood on the corner and he protected you. It was much less complicated than it is now. No one could touch you. You gave so much as a peep and they all were there. Now you have to call the police if something happens and no one wants to do that because of the problems it creates with our licences".

"Look," says Monique. "In the past if you wanted to work, you went by somewhere and if there was a room available you showed your passport one time and could start working immediately. That was easy for everyone. Now we have to register everyone, you have to have an intake interview and everyday you have to show your passport. Even if you have worked here for years".

I think back to the past. With mixed feelings about some things. We had fun and it was our lifestyle, there's no point in whining about that later. But looking at it from today's perspective definitely not everything was okay. Jan knows exactly what was going on on the canal and completes my thoughts: "The boys drove along the canals with their gold chains and fancy cars to deliver their girls. Out in the open for all to see and no one had a problem with it. There were a few nice guys among them too, and the women were perfectly capable of looking after themselves. Okay, occasionally someone was slapped around if they didn't feel like working, but that's the way it was. This is the work they wanted to do and they also wanted to see their man driving a nice car. I'm not blind you know, I am very aware of what's going on. But it's not so different from what goes on in the rest of the world".

Monique says that one of the women who has worked the last fifteen years from one of their rooms was so fed up that she wrote a letter to the Mayor. In it she wrote: 'What do you mean that window prostitution is a thing of the past? In fact it's exactly of this time because everyone who wants to can do it. It doesn't matter how old you are or how you look. I chose to do this, I want to be seen and I am proud of my body.' Jan sighs and says: "Actually there's no point to any of that. When one of the women writes a letter you hear through the grapevine that it's assumed they did it because we told them to. Neither they nor the women take us seriously. I am willing to go to bat for all the women who currently rent from us. Not one of them is forced to do this work. It could really be happening in the neighbourhood, but not that I am aware of. If the police are so certain that someone is being forced to work somewhere, then they need to do something about that. That's their job by the way.

About how busy it is on the street is also something. It's only busy one or two days, it's totally blown out of proportion.

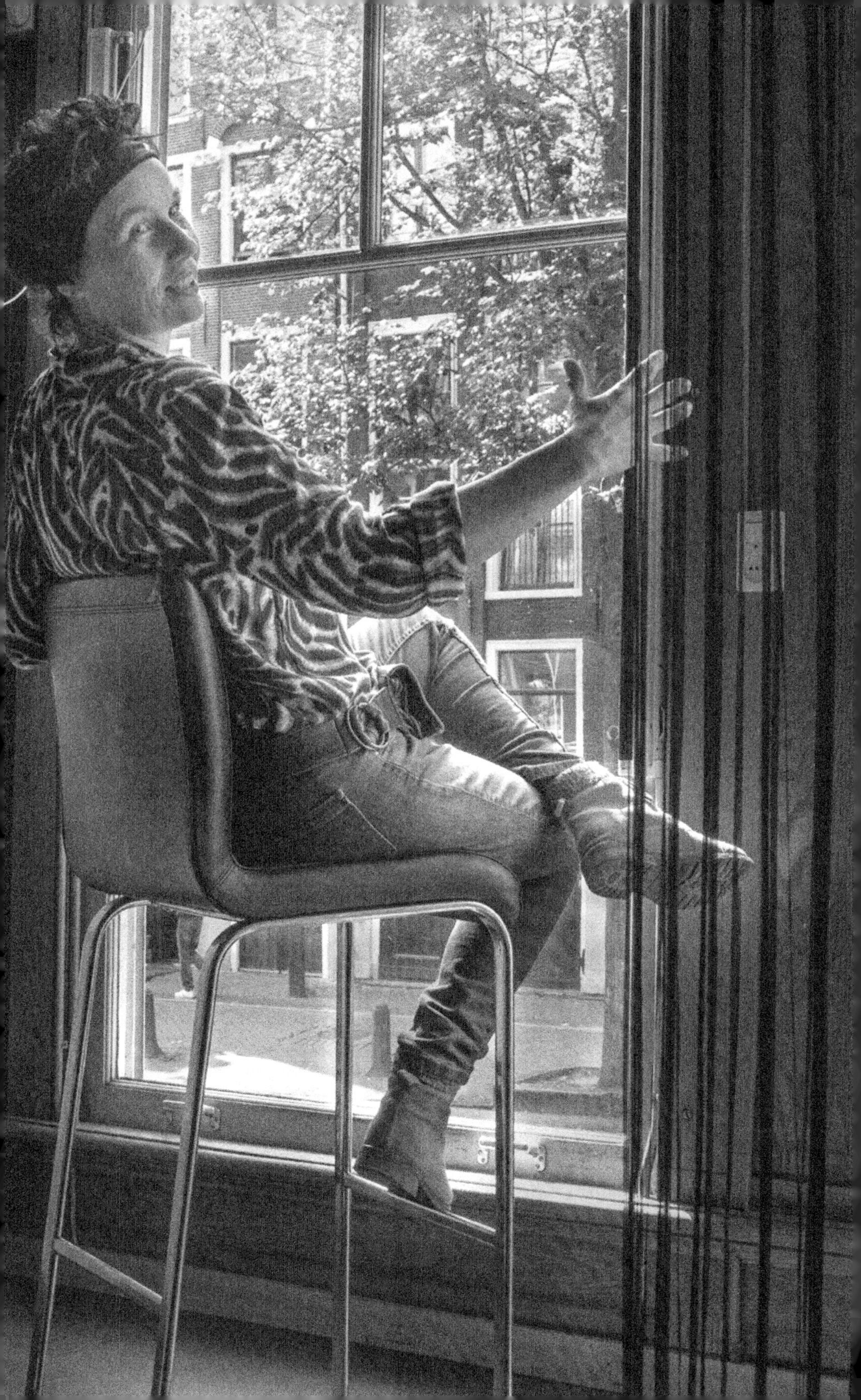

Sure, at some spots it can be busy, but the city has created this by allowing more bars and restaurants into the area. The cafe terraces are next to the window brothels so the women can't carry out their normal work anymore. Not only the women but also the brothel owners. They're been driven so crazy that they want to stop and sell the buildings. That's exactly what the city wants.

What I want? I don't want things to change. Everything should just stay the way it is. What I do want to see changed is the reputation of the neighbourhood. The media and politicians deliberately put the Wallen in a negative light. Reports present false statistics and lies – about how much crime is going on here – without any evidence. That has to stop. They should be proud of the neighbourhood and tell the public that things are properly organised here. Because it is. Instead, they want to get rid of us. But I don't want to go away. Where am I supposed to go?"

Before we leave I want to show Robin the upstairs room with the big window. Jan and Monique's beautiful, long-haired cats follow us up the stairs. The youngest of the two jumps up onto the stool behind the window and poses for us. "A pussy behind the window!" Robin giggles, grasping the double-meaning of the moment before I do. I immediately recognise the window and the view. Robin takes photos. Mainly of the pussy sitting on the stool behind the window.

"I don't think that you were just a normal seventeen year old then," Robin says when I ask her later what she though about seeing my old workroom. "I thought it was cool, but there's no way I could see myself at that age doing that. I think we are very different in that way. When I was seventeen I was still very childish. I was a bit of a house mouse, went to school and had just gotten my first job. If I have trouble with it? Why would I have trouble with something that I have known my whole life. I thought it was pretty crazy when I was sixteen and realised that you were that old when you started doing this work. I thought: How is that even possible"?

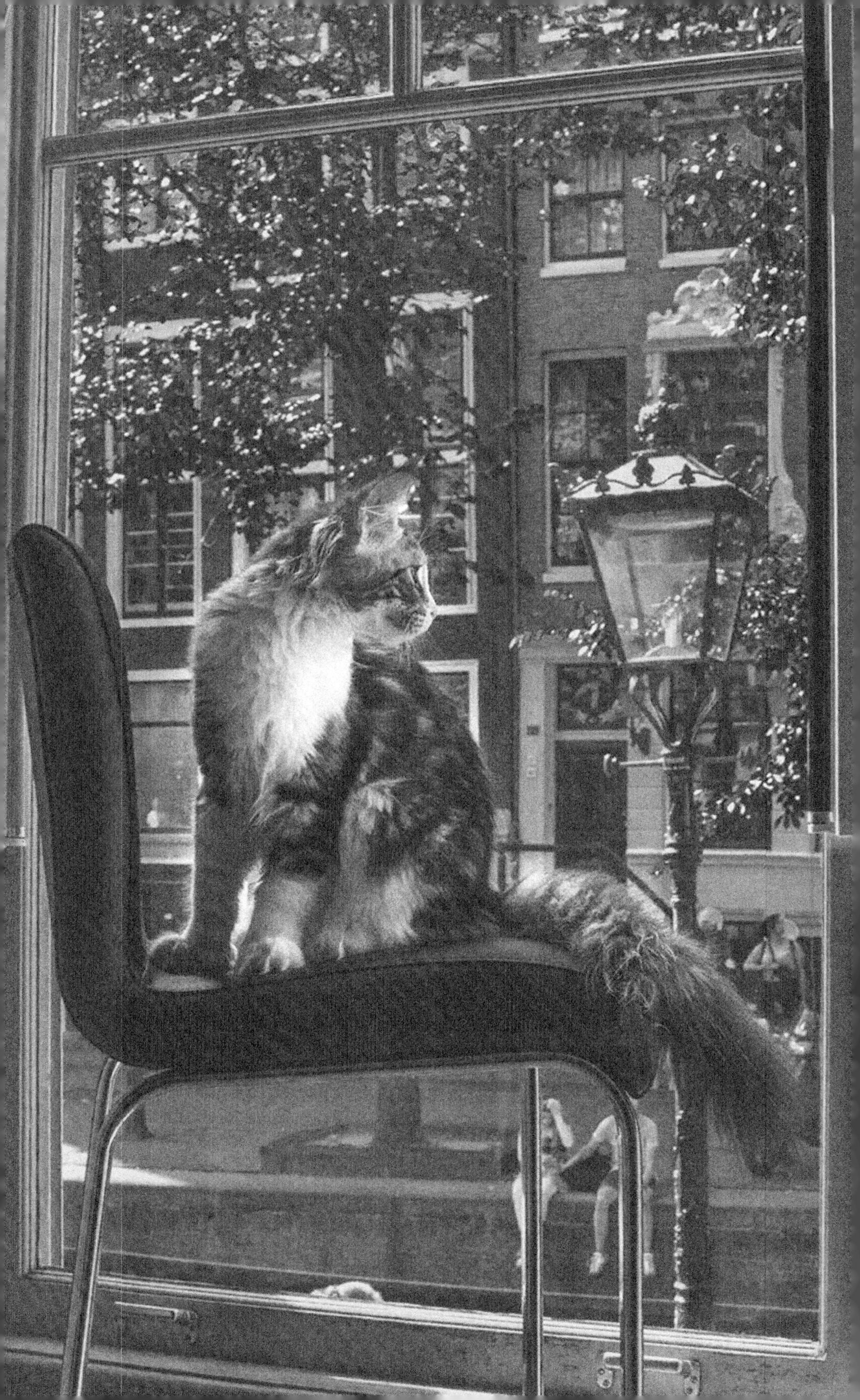

Schmidt's wood shop located across from my old window has existed since 1862. I have purchased many a red lightbulb and other hardware there. Joop has worked here for almost forty years and I ask him if he still enjoys working in the Wallen after all this time. "Yes," he answers wholeheartedly, "All sorts come in here. People who maintain the brothels or pubs and people who live here. You came here once because the key broke off in your front door and you couldn't open it. This is still a very old neighbourhood. The longer you work here, the more people you get to know. I've seen them come and go. It doesn't feel different to me. There's a good feeling here and we just do our work". By chance Joop's wife drops in as she's in the neighbourhood. "Nah, she's never uneasy," Joop laughs. "As a child she lived really close by so she really knows the area well". It wasn't long after our chat that it we heard that Schmidt's would be closing. The building on the Oudezijds Achterburgwal has been offered to the city for the purpose of monitoring the neighbourhood. The plan is to set up a neighbourhood post that can be used by city inspectors as well as the police. A good plan. I am curious. It's such a shame though that the neighbourhood will have to do without a wood shop from next year.

It's often said that the Wallen is unique because of the different functions and activities. That's true. There really are some differences between the types of businesses that have gradually established themselves here over the years – a sort of organic evolution – and functions which have been pushed into spaces in order to impose change. On the other side of the canal for example is now a row of new businesses, all of them in a former window brothel. The buildings stood empty for a couple of years after being used temporarily by artists and fashion designers, until small businesses were found that the city felt fit the picture better. I decide to visit one soon.

"It is 1995. Gigolos are a hot topic in the media. Where is this coming from now? I am intrigued and curious about what would happen if there were men standing behind the windows in the Wallen for female clients. I place an advertisement in the newspaper seeking men who would like to do this for a day and I ask my neighbour if I can rent a couple of windows a little further up on the Oudekerksplein. No problem. I will compensate the women who normally work there for lost income. The PIC's telephone hasn't stopped ringing. I ask the serious callers to send a photo and short letter of motivation. The search is hilarious: 'He's hot, and I wouldn't do it with him if it were for free'. Sometimes I find myself behaving just like some of the men here on the street and am shocked at how easily I can make these kinds of comments. Finally the day arrives. I ask the media not to come film or take photographs, but I knew in advance that this would fall on deaf ears. My fault, this kind of experiment is just too juicy. The following day a newspaper publishes pictures of the men behind the windows that were secretly taken from the public urinal across the canal. A few of the Latin American window prostitutes from the area go an try the men out. "Now it's our turn," they call out. Tante Mein is not impressed and angrily calls AT5, a local new agency. 'Men don't belong behind the windows, they have to pay! Get lost!' In the afternoon, Ton van Rooyen from AT5 races over with his camera crew causing a commotion and we end up closing the curtains earlier than we had wanted to. It was a fun experiment, but the neighbourhood isn't ready for it yet".

Talking about sex, how?

Talking to your daughter about sex if you are a (ex)prostitute, is not necessarily easy. People expect someone whose work involves sex to know everything and to be able to communicate well with their children about it, but it's not that simple. It's just like a psychiatrist whose private life is a mess. Everything that works in the treatment context and the advice they give to clients isn't helpful when it's about their own problems. Personal emotions change everything. I always wanted to act as normal as possible when it came to sex(work) and answer questions when they came up. But I also had to be careful about what I said. I don't always talk so positive about men and needed to watch out about giving too much information. I am afraid I haven't quite succeeded in that.

If you grow up with a sex positive attitude – an expression I find important, which I learned from Ine Vanwesenbeeck, Professor of Sexual Development, Diversity and Health – It can be easier for you to respect the preferences and choices of others along with your own.

Sex workers often have a positive, self assured attitude when it comes to sexuality. But the struggle between radical and liberal feminisms makes it difficult for the rest of the world. Within radical feminist ideology, women in pornography or prostitution are per definition victims of violence and exploitation. Radical feminists are so-called sex negative and have a lot in common with Christian political parties. They have had a lot of hidden influence on people's perception of the Wallen, which both regard as a kind of portal to hell. On top of that, we now have the 'Me Too generation' who are more aware of their rights and who find all forms of sexual transgression increasingly unacceptable. In principle that's good, but it has also led to an even more critical gaze regarding sex work, and specifically window prostitution.

"I often listened when you gave a lecture," Robin says. "That's how I learned my first English words. Although I didn't understand most of it. What did I know what a 'blowjob' was. Did I actually ever ask?" I tell her that I don't remember and feel myself slowly turning red. That wasn't exactly an example I would have wanted to share myself. Without my being aware of it, she would have seen and heard enough when she was a child that perhaps I would have wanted to avoid or convey differently. As far as I know I never spoke very explicitly about sexual acts. I did talk about safety, standing up for yourself and setting boundaries. I thought that was more important. You don't learn about sexual positions and acts from you mother. That's something you learn through doing or you ask your girlfriends and your best friend Google.

Of course we talked often and in detail about condoms. I showed her how to put one on, using a plastic model of a penis that I had from the city health department, and she also practised once on a banana. I would consider myself very fortunate if I could see to it that Robin can stand up for herself and not end up in bad relationships out of insecurity. That was the plan. I had a sort of mantra: 'No one has the right to touch you if you don't want them to'. In hindsight I think that I may have emphasised that too much.

"I did know a lot about saying yes or no and about condoms when I was still young," Robin says with a laugh. "Maybe I was just a little too good at saying no. Everyone always thought I was a late bloomer, but I just always said no. There was a period in elementary school that I drew pictures of people having sex. I think that I had seen them on postcards. The interest was there, but it was only later that I understood that you could also have sex for pleasure and with feeling. I was actually quite confused because I had learned early on that for some people sex is work. I had difficulty differentiating between sex for love and sex as your job and so I wanted nothing to do with it in the beginning. Rationally I always understood the difference, but it confused me emotionally. It was only after friends started sharing their sexual experiences with me that I learned that you could also have sex for fun. And luckily everything turned out fine".

> "It is 1984. I haven't been working for very long. I like it here in the private brothel. The Wallen hasn't entered my mind yet and I am still saying 'that I would never lower myself by standing behind a window'. In a year I think differently about that. When there is a client for me I get paged and then jump on my bike. Sometimes my boss, Jan, comes to pick me up. They choose me from a photo album. It works great because then I can do my own thing the rest of the day. Most of my clients are older men, but then at my age pretty much everyone is 'older', so that's not saying much. I don't care. It's not about the sex, it's work. As crazy as it sounds, I could just as well be doing the dishes. Some clients want to cuddle or kiss. I don't do any of that. That's reserved for my private life. I am not the greatest at this job, but also not bad. It's easy for me and I have no problem differentiating between my work and personal life. Call it a natural talent. Or deviation. Interpret it however you like. The outside world calls me a whore, without realising that they are talking about me. I don't fit the picture. When I am feeling cynical I sometimes ask myself if there is something wrong with me, because actually, I'm really okay with that picture".

We walk a block to the left through the Monnikenstraat, the Gordijnensteeg and the Bloedstraat. The street name Gordijnensteeg (Curtain lane) is really quite apt given the curtains in the window brothels there, but that is not what It refers to. It was simply the family name of the people who used to live there. The other two street names refer to the Grauwemonnikenklooster, a (Greyfriars) monastery that was established here around 1500. Many historians mention a 'bloedkamer (blood room)' that was possibly used as an operating theatre or torture chamber. That does give the name Bloedstraat a bit of sinister significance. Sometimes painful looking implements hang in a window brothel in the Bloedstraat from women who also offer sadomasochistic services. With the story of a possible torture chamber in the monastery in the back of my mind, I can really appreciate these kind of unconscious coincidences. As if the past is playfully trying to harmonise with the present. Robin thinks it's 'cool shit'.

In the last years the Bloedstraat has become known for the transgender sex workers who work there. For clients it's convenient to know where you can find what you are looking for. On the other hand, this knowledge can sometimes also be annoying for everyone working there because it can provoke a certain behaviour. On top of that, cisgender women also work here. It's a very gender diverse street and can be painful when you are approached as someone you are not. Within our circle of friends and acquaintances, Robin and I know several people who have transitioned. I have absolutely no difficulty with that. Why would you? I think it would be difficult and unimaginable to feel that you are in the wrong body, but living in a world that mocks you and is intolerant, now that's truly awful.

Robin agrees and says that she wouldn't even know how to answer someone who asks her what she thinks about transsexuality. "I don't understand why anyone would have any difficulty with it. It's something that I have learned a lot about in the last couple of years, thanks for our travels and connections. Something I still find complicated in relation to sex work, is when someone is transitioning from a man to a women, but chooses not to go through all the surgeries because then they may get fewer clients. I find that interesting. I get it but then also not. Then because of your work it means you can't totally become yourself. I think that must be difficult".

I remember who we can ask and we go to visit Anaisa. She is very open about how it all went for her.

"I was eighteen and had just begun transitioning," she tells us. "I didn't really know what to do with myself. I left home and ended up in the Wallen because I was looking for a place to sleep. I didn't know then that transsexuals could also work here. I had seen them, but I thought that they had all their surgeries. I had just begun hormone treatment myself.

In the Bloedstraat I went up to someone and asked her if she was transsexual. She was mad at me for asking, until I said that was too and only wanted to know if I could work if I hadn't had surgery yet. Then she shifted her skirt just a little and showed me what she had there. I was surprised. We stayed in touch and once in a while she called me to work with her if a client requested a threesome. At that time you didn't have to register with the Chamber of Commerce in order to be able to work here, so I could try things out stress-free. At some point I started working for real, in the Barndesteeg. My plan was to work for a short while and save some money, but now it's eight years later and I am still here.

I found it really scary in the beginning and stood there shaking. All those people looking at you. You never really get used to it. If I've been gone for a bit, then the first two days back I am shaking again. Right now I work in an upper room and that's better. I never want to stand on street level again. The people are much too close by and it makes me feel vulnerable. I can defend myself fine you know, but sometimes I am too nice. Despite being nervous in the beginning, all the attention makes me really feel like a bit of a diva. I love it. People looking at me and thinking I am beautiful. I enjoy my work.

The only option for me is working behind the window. I also wouldn't want to work in another city or even in another neighbourhood. I am used to it here and I also feel safe. Safer here even than in the neighbourhood where I live. We all know each other here. It isn't always fun, but it is my family. If there's a problem, we help each other. In my community we all have the same background and because of that we support each other. There are not only transsexuals working in the Bloedstraat. I don't call myself that anymore now that I have had all my surgeries. At some point I found it unnecessary. I am a woman. Cross-dressers, transsexuals who have not had surgery and transwomen like me who have completely transitioned, all work here in our street.

I think it's the nicest street in the neighbourhood, but people are really pretty rude. Especially towards the cross-dressers working on street level. They really get verbally abused and laughed at. It's really annoying, but I don't think you can really do much about it. It happens everywhere. When she walks through the Bijenkorf, she'll also be laughed at. That's just the way people are. If you can't take it, then you shouldn't come and work here. Some friends, who have had surgery and are totally female, work on the canal among the other women. I could do that too but I earn good money here and actually I'm not interested in standing where it's so busy. Because I stand in this street, I sometimes get asked if I am transsexual and then I say no. Even if that is what clients are looking for. When I hadn't had my operation yet, I told them of course, but that's when being transsexual was still part of the way I worked. I really had to get used to that after. But shortly before my last operation I was already so feminine that people couldn't tell anymore.

I made almost no money anymore because men thought that I was a woman. So my type of client didn't come to me anymore because I looked too female and others clients wouldn't come in once they learned that I didn't have a vagina. After the operation everything became much easier because now I am completely female.

People in the neighbourhood are nervous. The discussion that keeps circulating about windows closing is causing a lot of tension. You don't know where you stand. A lot of my colleagues really would have no idea what they would do if they couldn't do this work anymore. A couple trans-colleagues from other countries have even given up their apartments and work as much as possible because they are afraid that the windows will be shut down. They want to get what they can while it's still possible. But they can't just shut us down like that? I can't imagine that the windows will be gone one day. I have thought about what I would do if the windows were relocated, but I really don't see myself working somewhere in an industrial area. I love this neighbourhood and the atmosphere here. Even the tourists. Once in a while I get tired of it all and can't handle seeing another man. Then I take a few weeks off. But after a while I get bored to death and want to start again. If work was taken away from me, I don't know what I would do. It's all I've got.

For me, I don't think working with closed curtains is an option. Then I would prefer to pay a hundred and seventy euro a night for a hotel room with a jacuzzi and solicit clients there. Why would I sit here behind a window with the curtains closed? I think that's so weird.

I think that the city should really support us instead of saying that they want to help us and then just coming up with more regulations. They could do that by ensuring that everyone doing this work can take a normal vacation and that all of the rooms are properly maintained. Luckily that's all taken care of where I work, but I there are enough colleagues where that's not the case. Workers who have to continue to pay rent when they are not working and whose workrooms are a mess. You pay almost two hundred euro per night in rent and then it's dirty. That shouldn't be allowed, right?

Or girls who want to stop but can't find any other work or affordable housing so they have to keep working to pay the rent. The existing exit programs don't help with that. It's even more difficult for transsexuals to find other work. It is a vicious circle that you can't get out of and what the city is doing now is only causing stress. Then you have to go here for papers and then back there again for a licence. How does that help us?

I don't know about that plan for a prostitution hotel. If they put it outside of the city centre, I don't see much in it. If it's designed like the Pascha in Germany – where there are also windows and a club inside – then it might work. But that people who work out of their homes need a licence, I don't think that's right. There are so many people who have a another life and do this work on the side for a little extra money. They would never apply for a licence. It's just too risky that the people around you will find out what you do. The trans-community in sex work is a separate world. The community has its own communication channels and some earn a lot of money. We have a different kind of clientele. I found it difficult at times. The clients have a sort of fantasy and most would say they are straight. They find it really titillating, but once it's over that's it. Then suddenly they don't want to be touched anymore. That's pretty hurtful. And that's not something that just happens in sex work, it's also like that in the daily lives of transsexuals.

I have another type of client since my transition. Now I have the real men, finally! My clients used to come to me in secret; wearing a hoodie and alone. Now they come with their friends and walk out all cool, ready for their applause afterwards. I seriously enjoy that. When I open the curtain again I really get a kick. There's nothing degrading about that. I feel just like an entertainer. I get it that there are colleagues who might not like that but for me it's a confirmation of my femaleness. We don't need any help really. I have this neighbourhood and my work. If they take that away from me, then I'll need help ".

"It is 1985. I meet someone in a disco. After closing time we go to the Casablanca on the Zeedijk. We dance. What do you do for your work?, he asks. 'Oh', I say. 'Um, I work as a secretary.' He starts laughing. Do you believe that yourself? I laugh with him and stop talking. A few weeks later he's at my house and my pager goes off. It's the boss at the private brothel. Grabbing the telephone I realise that it could come out now. One of my regulars is asking for me, and if I can come. I agree and notice my boyfriend looking at me with curiosity. I tell him about my work. His eyes twinkle. I am young and rebellious and I have a big mouth. But I also feel insecure. I don't understand much about life yet. I just think it's complicated. At least at work everything is clear. It's not always good, but it is what it is. Everything is straightforward and that I understand. The boyfriend is a thug. He is strong and dominating but I don't care. I feel a little uneasy but it's exciting. Bring it on. I'll see where it takes me".

Almost all of my colleagues in the old neighbourhood had a 'friend'. We called them our men. We were their woman. They just hung around on the street while we were working or brought and picked us up. In between things they did odd jobs. Sometimes legal, mostly not. After work we all went to drink something or dance at Zorba the Buddha on the Oudezijds Voorburgwal. The men felt just as attracted to the lifestyle of the Wallen as we did. We were sort of doomed to find each other. They had no interest in a nice girl and we had no interest in an upstanding office type. The relationships weren't always equal but we weren't bothered by that. At least not all the time.

When I worked in the Wallen, there was only one time that I has a policeman at my door asking to see my passport. I didn't even have one yet so I gave him the name of a colleague who was already eighteen. There were no consequences and no questions were asked. At the time that was great, but in retrospect a little too easy. My boyfriend could arrange a window for me and people thought that was totally normal too.

Things changed drastically when the new regulations came in. It was a new era. At the rental agency La Vie en Rose they hung a big sign on the stairs saying 'no cowboys', making it clear that boyfriends or other third parties were no longer welcome.

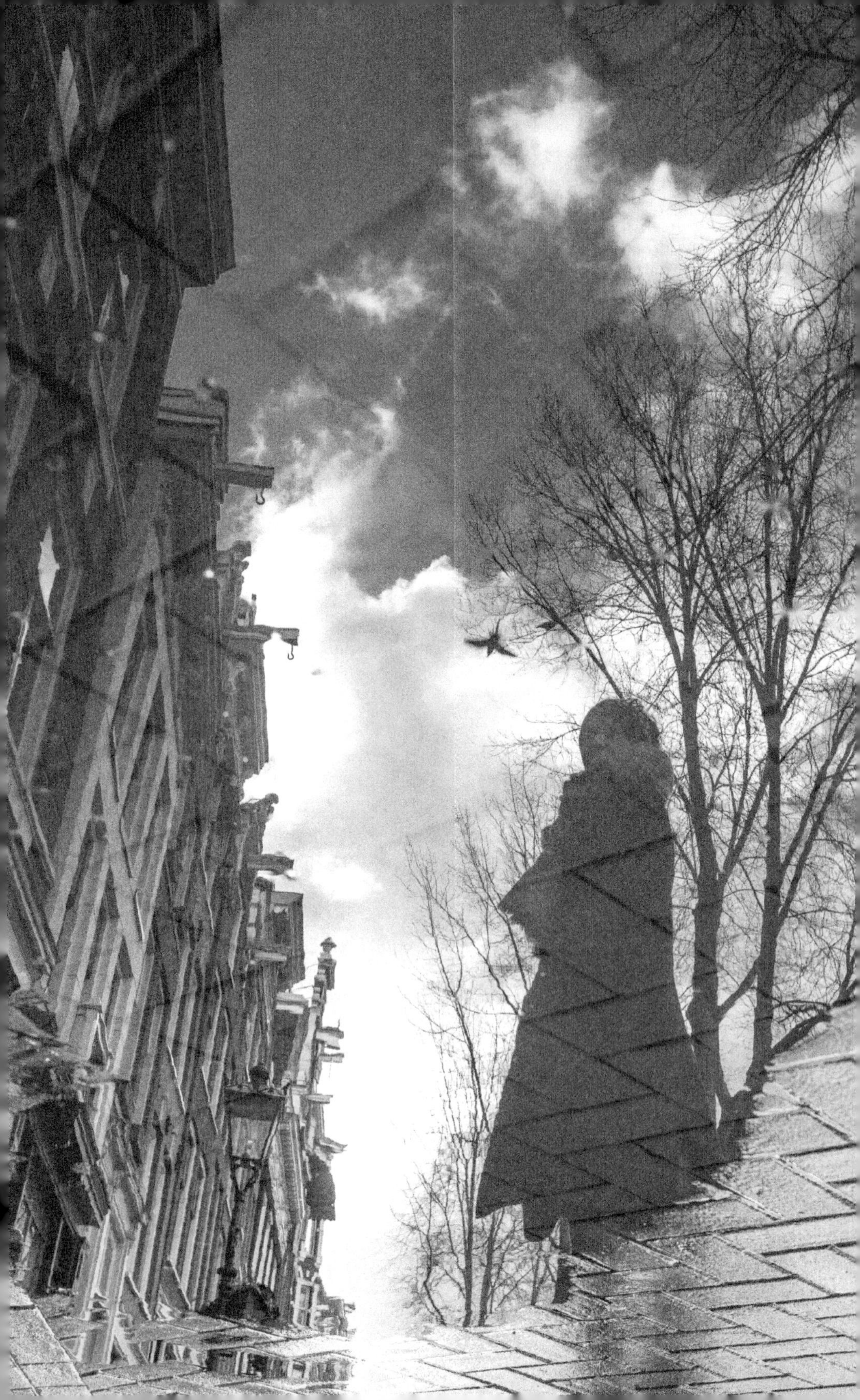

The city informed window brothel owners that the women had to personally come and arrange things themselves. Pimps slowly faded from the street scene. Since then, the responsibility for safety falls to the window brothels owners and the sex workers themselves. Every window brothel has a panic button and if you press it an alarm goes off either in the rental office or on the street. A lot of the windows already had an outside alarm, often also with a flashing light. Because brothel owners these day risk getting a citation if there are problems, some will only call the police as a last resort. Strict government brothel regulations are no guarantee of safety and can even be counterproductive. Still, the Wallen doesn't feel unsafe. Alarms rarely go off, there aren't many street fights these days and break-ins and muggings don't happen often. What you do need to watch out for are pickpockets and street dealers, often selling fake drugs. But that goes for the whole of the city centre.

"In general safety is pretty good", says sex worker Anaisa. "One time I had a very violent client. After that I was more careful, especially in the way I approach them. When there is a conflict and you start screaming, things can really escalate. If you can stay calm then it usually works out fine. For me that fifty euro is just not worth getting slapped around for so if it happens that a client is not satisfied, I give the money back. I was way more 'getto' in the past and there was no way I would give money back. Not happy? Too bad. That one violent experience opened my eyes to the situation. It didn't change the way I felt about my work but it was a reality check. Getting robbed or punched in the face could also happen if you worked at a supermarket".

> "It is 1985. I like my work fine but my relationship is complicated. My boyfriend takes his pimp role, that I just passively accepted, too serious and his thug lifestyle is also getting a little out of hand. This evening we were visiting friends. Just before eight he motioned to the clock saying it was time for us to go, but I was really enjoying myself and didn't want to leave. We were both getting on each other's nerves and in anger I suddenly yelled: 'God damn it, why don't you go and stand behind the window yourself!' Furious, he grabbed me by my hair and dragged me into the hall. At the top of the stairs I tried to fight him off, until he put his gun to my head. At that point things got pretty hysterical, eventually

ending with me going to work as usual. I stand there with a long face so I probably won't earn much tonight. He stands on the corner looking as if everything is fine and feeling pretty full of himself. Frankly, I'm feeling a little over this".

"To me that situation is too bizarre to even be able to imagine," Robin says. "I know the background to this story and also see how it got this far. I get how this could have happened because I know and understand you, but when you first told me about this I was really shocked. Even though I know you're not dumb, I think that you haven't always made the best choices. I would have done things differently. But my life is different than yours was at that time and so I don't see myself ending up in those kinds of situations."

We cross the bridge by the Stoofsteeg and walk in the direction of the most noteworthy sex theatre in the Wallen: the Casa Rosso. Just to pop in to say hi to Jan. When he sees me coming, he regularly shouts: "That's going to cost me again!" And he's not wrong. For years he has been the most important sponsor of many projects; mine and others. On more than one occasion I have stood with him in the ticket booth and seen how people came one after the other to ask for help or sponsorship money. Even the neighbourhood dogs drag their owners inside to get a treat. The dogs always get something, but Jan Otten is tougher on the others these days. Sometimes I get the idea that he thinks I'm a pain in the ass, but I know he likes to tease. Once he told me: "If I had known back then that you were working there, I would have dragged you out". He doesn't have anything against prostitution, but he does have a problem with girls who are too young working behind the window. Even if I thought differently about that at the time myself. Jan doesn't tolerate the slightest injustice.

His usual spot is next to the entrance of the theatre, where he can mess with passers-by by spraying them with water from the trunk of an elephant that hangs on the front of the theatre and making really crude comments, but he has a heart of gold. To get to know Jan better, I highly recommend the book 'Casa Rosso' by Rob van Hulst. "It's a great book about ordinary things," Jan says. "The publisher really wanted it to be more sensational because that sells better, but then I would have had to name names and I don't do that. It's just like in Las Vegas: everything that happens in the Casa Rosso, stays in the Casa Rosso". Jan's imperium, which includes the Banana Bar, the Erotic Museum and the peep show, wasn't spared by Project 1012. Because Jan couldn't get any financing from a bank he went to his friend Charrel – who the city claims is shady – and that brought his licences into question. Fortunately everything worked out. "I'm proud of my business and I work hard," Jan says. "When we were kids Charrel and I would walk hand-in-hand to visit the Artis Zoo. I come from a poor family and I ate at his house almost everyday. He's more to me than a friend or brother. When I wanted to buy the Casa Rosso, he lent me the money. The bank would have never given to me.

All the women here in the neighbourhood are just the sweetest. I have absolutely nothing against them. How could I, I am one of them. You have to be an Amsterdammer to understand this neighbourhood. In the last few years a lot of new people have moved into this area and they are all outsiders. There are almost no complaints on this section of the canal where it's the busiest, but in other, quieter sections the people who live there complain the most. Those people don't know anything about our business and have nothing to do with it. Naturally, I see drunk people, but I don't have much trouble here with that. It helps that I have security everywhere, but if you know that works then you should have more security present in the neighbourhood. More police would also help but they are not around either. I hired more security to keep things quiet out front. The guys tell me that everyone warns them that 'if they have to work in the Wallen, they better wear a bulletproof vest,' or 'you're going to get knifed in the back'. Actually they like the work and nothing happens. Having them around acts as a deterrent. Too many stories about the neighbourhood are totally crazy, lies or exaggerated to make it seem more exciting.

Actually there two parallel discussions going on. One concerns prostitution, but I have nothing to do with that. I made a comment about it in the past once and was asked by the brothel owner Jan Broers why I was sticking my nose in things. He's right. My business is erotic entertainment and that's different. I don't get involved in the discussion about prostitution. But the other discussion is about the neighbourhood and that's very close to my heart. My children are proud of what their father does. That's because I am proud of it myself. On Saturday afternoons in the past I would walk through the neighbourhood with my wife and youngest daughter and we would go by the peep show on the Oudekerksplein that was still open then. One time my daughter remarked: 'Wow, Katja can really dance well'. She had been just watching along on the monitor. Sometimes I see people walking with a hand covering their children's eyes. Why walk here then? You know what your going to see here. That's something that I have always been very aware of. You won't see anything in the photos that hang here outside. It's the same with the whole neighbourhood. You imagine all kinds of things, but it's all in your head".

"It is 1988. I shifted from working in the Wallen to a private brothel on the Overtoom. The money isn't so great, but at least I don't have to pay rent and it is pretty relaxed. We have a cosy lounge area where we all sit and when clients come you go one after the other to introduce yourself. Then you go with the client to a separate room for a half hour or hour. That's quite a bit longer than I am used to. In the Wallen they were usually gone after fifteen minutes. All the chitchat that's involved is really not my thing. I miss the independence that I had behind the window and the work tempo. Better more clients quickly than a couple for a longer time. But really, for now this is better. I am back to school again at the night school on the Leidseplein. I can do my homework here during the day. If I ever become a mother, I don't want to feel ashamed in front of my child because I never even finished high school. I stay and eat here sometimes and then we cook for ourselves. Recently I saw a client in between peeling potatoes. That's pretty hilarious. My parents and I are back in touch. They helped my find an apartment and are happy that I am going to school. It's better that they don't know what else I am doing".

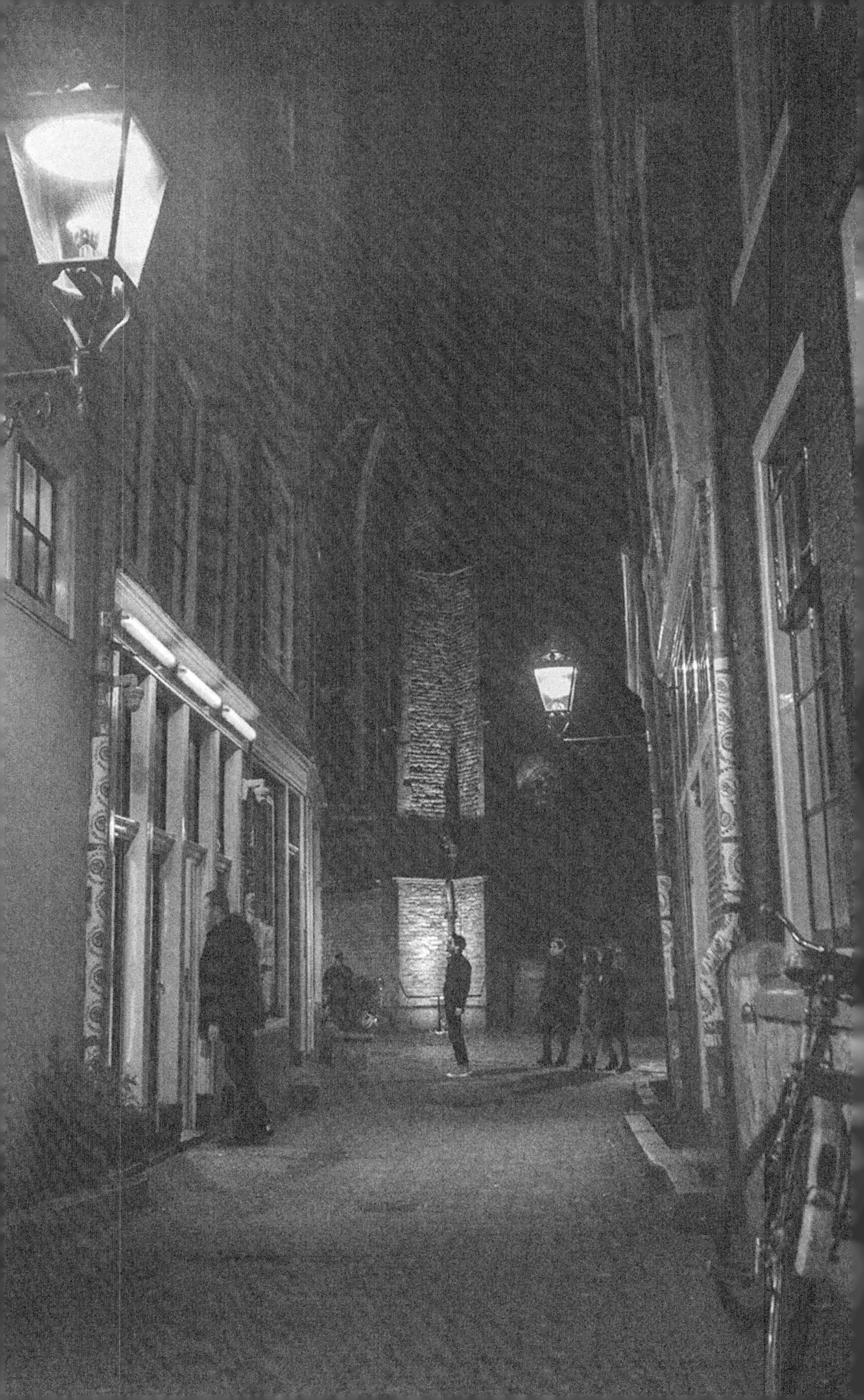

"People often ask me how I would feel if you decided to do the same work," I say to Robin. "It's a pretty annoying question, but I understand where it comes from. Do they sometimes ask you the same?"

"I don't think it's such a crazy question you know," Robin says. "You always say that we shouldn't make such a big deal of it. It might not be the most normal job you can think of, but it's not the craziest either. I'm glad that you give me the space to do what I want to do and I know that you would respect my choice if I ever decided to do sex work. Although I also know that would be with mixed feelings. I have thought about it and asked myself if I could ever do it. Especially on days where I really can use some money. But I know all the things that I would have to deal with and I don't think I could handle it. There's no way I could do it secretly. I wouldn't want to and you know what a terrible liar I am. I don't like secrets. I would find it difficult having sex with people who are not always so respectful. But at the job I have now people are sometimes unkind to me too. Okay, it's different if you don't have any clothes on, but then the other guy doesn't either, right? I have talked about it with a friend. Don't look so worried, I am not saying that I am going to do it. You are always so protective, it's annoying man…I only think that I could do it. I inherited that entrepreneurial spirit from you and dad; that independent streak and taking matters in your own hands. Sex workers have that mentality and I do too. I am really glad that you never kept it a secret from me. I think I would be really angry if you had just told me now. Then it really hurts. Not because of the work, but because you kept something secret from me for years. That's not necessary if you have a good relationship with each other. If you start working again I think that's fine. I would keep a closer eye on you, because I also inherited your protectiveness. Damn it".

"It is 2006. For the first time I am organising an Open Day in the Wallen. Almost everyone is participating. You can visit many of the businesses in the neighbourhood for free. You can stand behind the window, see the peep show, go into the church or go into and look around peoples homes. At the Casa Rosso there are long lines of people who would normally never go there. Nice ladies want to give sitting on a stool behind the window a try. Over and over they shriek: "Oh, this isn't so bad at all' and 'it's really quite nice here'. Someone's grandmother learns how to roll a joint at the Bulldog. Another person sits carefully on the bed in a window brothel. 'The light switch is in a really odd place,' someone says, pointing to the alarm button by the headboard. I almost die laughing when I suddenly see my mother standing behind a window. It's good that people can come and have a look behind the scenes. That they learn how it all works, get to know the people and that they learn to see the neighbourhood more as 'normal'. Not that they all have to start doing sex work now, but these kind of events help to build a more positive image. That is good for everyone".

We come to the part of the canal that's across from the Schmidt's wood shop, where a lot of new small businesses occupy what were once window brothels. I go up the stairs to Red Light Ice, an ice cream and waffle shop. Now It's one of many waffle shops in the city centre, but this was the first according to owner Shab. Eight years ago he was able to rent the space. Through Project 1012, it was possible for a friend of his to register his interest in a commercial space in the Wallen. Together they submitted a business proposal, which was approved. It seems that an ice cream and waffle shop – with all due respect – is high quality enough to replace a window brothel. "For two years business was good," says Shab, "but then the concept was copied. In the meantime the city has created so many regulations to discourage this type of business, that sales have plummeted".

I share how I feel concerning the so-called higher value businesses in former window brothels and how tired I am that they choose a business name that refers to the Red Light District while the reason they were selected was to inject a new vibe into the neighbourhood. Shab says he understands that, but explains that the name is also logical given the location, which I also get. Any entrepreneur would jump at the chance to start a business in a unique location. It's pretty upsetting for him that his concept isn't unique anymore and that now he himself is experiencing what the brothels, whose place he took over, went through. Now it's ice cream and waffle shops that no longer fit into the picture.

We turn left and go into the Oudekennissteeg and go to visit with Tonia. After the room I had on the Oudezijds Achterburgwal, I moved to this street and rented from Bob and Tonia. Bob has passed away, but Tonia, formerly from the Jordaan neighbourhood, still lives here in the Wallen.

"Yes, I remember you very well," Tonia says. "I also remember your former boyfriend well. That was a special one. He really liked a fight. After, you would be standing working again as if nothing had happened. There wasn't any license requirement yet back then. Normally if a new girl wanted to come work, we had to bring her passport to the police station and they would register her. But that didn't happen all the time and they didn't control it so strictly either. I don't actually know why this didn't happen for you. It was partly because of the group you hung around with. They said that you were okay and never caused trouble. After two days I had seen it all: you were no angel.

I came to the Wallen fifty-four years ago. I met Bob when he lived above a cigar store. You knew it as the Alessandro Lunchroom. He was twenty-seven years older than me and not the easiest man but always good to me. I knew nothing yet about life in the Wallen. Bob had a nightclub and brought in clients from the Rembrandtplein for the girls who were working above the club. I never delved into the rules and had no idea if any of it was legal, but it was a lot of fun. I made coffee and tea for everyone. After a couple of years the girls would stand by the front door and some time after that the window brothels came in. I carried on renting after Bob died. Until about five years ago when I lost interest and stopped.

I have never had a problem with my children in the neighbourhood. My daughter Petra did ask me why the girls stood there in a bra and I just told her that they entertained men there, were properly paid to do so, and because of that we could walk safely on the street. And she accepted that. You have to make up some kind of story, right. People used to say to me: 'I don't understand how you can let your children grow up here'. I said to them that it doesn't really matter if they grow up here or in Amsterdam-Zuid. People have a problem with prostitution. They are afraid that it's sets a bad example for children and are immediately negative. People simply have no idea about what happens here in neighbourhood. They all think oh dear…but it's not that bad. I have three children. A daughter with my first husband. My son Tonnie I found in the sandbox on the Zeedijk. His parents were heroin addicts and Henk's parents were alcoholics. Tonnie was 4.5 and Henk around eleven when Bob and I took them in. We were still living on the canal then and Bob always stood on the bridge. I think the neighbourhood was a lot nicer then, it was friendlier. If there was something, then you were there for each other. Now it's everyone for themselves and the government dictates what you can and cannot do. We are not allowed to do this anymore or that anymore. There have to be rules, don't get me wrong, but there are more and more.

A few weeks ago the weather was nice and I sat outside on the pavement by Royal Taste, across from the window brothel that I sometimes had to look after. The cafe terrace was full so I took my coffee and sat on the steps next door. A city inspector came by and told me: 'You can't sit here, it's a private residence.' I told him: 'I've lived here for fifty-four years, you don't have to tell me what I can and cannot do'. Also, those steps aren't in front of a house but a window brothel and no one was working at the time. He didn't see the difference. Then I said to him: 'Now that you're here. There are five drunks who sit by my front door sometimes and you guys just walk past without saying anything. If you could do something about that sometime'. Yeah, the discussions people are having these days. You know, I am not so worried about the future of the windows in the Wallen. It's such an old profession, it's never going to disappear. I'm not going anywhere either. They'll have to drag me out in a box with Andre Hazes playing. I don't care which song, except Holy City because that's what I used at Bob's funeral".

Tonia's example of a city inspector warning her because she was sitting on some steps says a lot. They play an important role on the street, but if an inspector can't tell the difference between a resident having a coffee and a drunk tourist, things are pretty bad. Opinions are divided about nuisance and how busy it is, but everyone has a point when they say that people don't have to behave so rudely and that they are fed up with drunken groups hanging out on their doorsteps. Especially in the evenings the small side streets are really busy. It was busy in the past, but back then it was mostly on Saturday nights.

"It is 1987. The Oudekennissteeg is so busy you could crowd surf. On the corner it's quiet. The boys are locked up. There's a lot of drama and I am feeling unsettled. I am staying with some people I know in the neighbourhood because we were evicted from our house. The police raided it and they made a complete mess of the place. The landlord was not pleased. A lot has happened in the last couple of weeks and I need to figure out what I am going to do. I'll keep working for now but maybe it's time to switch gears. I think I'll go to check out a private brothel in the city soon. Go back to how I worked when I started a few years ago. It will be less money, but then I will have more peace and quiet. The Wallen is so crazy right now. I need a break. My dog Santa is with me which Tonia wasn't so happy about because she sheds quite a bit. I have to quickly find a new place for myself so I can leave her at home while I work. I really have to hustle because I'm out of money. Maybe my rich advertising client will come by tonight. If I am lucky he stays and sleeps for an hour for a couple of hundred guilders while I massage his feet. I could really use that".

When we reach the bridge over the Oudezijds Voorburgwal we hang around for a bit again. From here you can see the original Bulldog coffee shop and next to it the Trompettersteeg, which is the second smallest street in the Wallen with windows. The smallest street is the Slaperssteeg. It's on the other side of the Oude Kerk. There haven't been any windows there for years and it's gated off now because too much nastiness went on there, especially at the time the area was still full of street prostitutes and dealers. It was a good place for muggings, using drugs or a quickie with a client. The entrance to the Oude Kerk is on this side of the square. I tell Robin that when her father and I got married we used the other entrance, by the church tower. We'll pass that in a bit. First we pop into the Koffieschenkerij cafe, where we agreed to meet Joep.

Joep de Groot was a community police officer in the Wallen from 1972 to 2002 and he can still be found here almost daily. Like a lot of people who worked or lived in the Wallen, it seems he just can't say goodbye. He grew up in Veenhuizen, in a government institution. "Among the thugs and the pimps," as he puts it. "The women from this neighbourhood came every Sunday to visit. Big women in high heels with towering hairdos. Of course I found that really interesting. There was a lot of crazy gossip about it and that's exciting for a kid. There's a saying, 'a pimp is made'. Well, I really did pity some of them, you know. Smartly dressed and a fancy car, but if they needed gas they had to go and ask mama. I've been through quite a lot in the neighbourhood. It was a really a mess in the old days. Old and dilapidated. It was full of cars because you could still park anywhere in those days and it was chock-full of large and small businesses. There were constant traffic jams. Back then prostitution was integrated with the neighbourhood. There were something like 250 rooms when I started working here and the control by vice police was strict. The ladies sat behind the window knitting with a cup of tea and their clothes buttoned high. They were registered and I believe they had to pay taxes. In the neighbourhood this was accepted. Once they went beyond the Wallen they were suddenly whores. They were also called whores in the neighbourhood, but there it had a different emphasis. They were important to the economy here. There were a lot of locals making money from the sex business: the brothel cleaners, the hairstylists on the Zeedijk – we had four – the coffee houses and the pubs. Prices were at least ten percent higher here than in other Amsterdam neighbourhoods. So-called whore prices.

The sailors would walk here from the East harbour to blow off steam. The neighbourhood changed as soon as the harbour was relocated to the west of the city. All of a sudden the pubs were quieter and the women had less work. In the eighties the area profited from the arrival of American soldiers. You probably also had them as clients. They were stationed in Germany and came here on weekends to party. They had money.

I started at the police academy in 1965. There was a lot going on in Amsterdam. The city was alive. It was an interesting time to join the police force. I did my training at the Warmoesstraat police station and later became a community police officer there. I felt responsible for my neighbourhood. As a community police officer you get to know people's personal situations. I am not so quick to judge because of this. There was a lot of laughter and drinking in the pubs, but in the background there was just as much sadness.

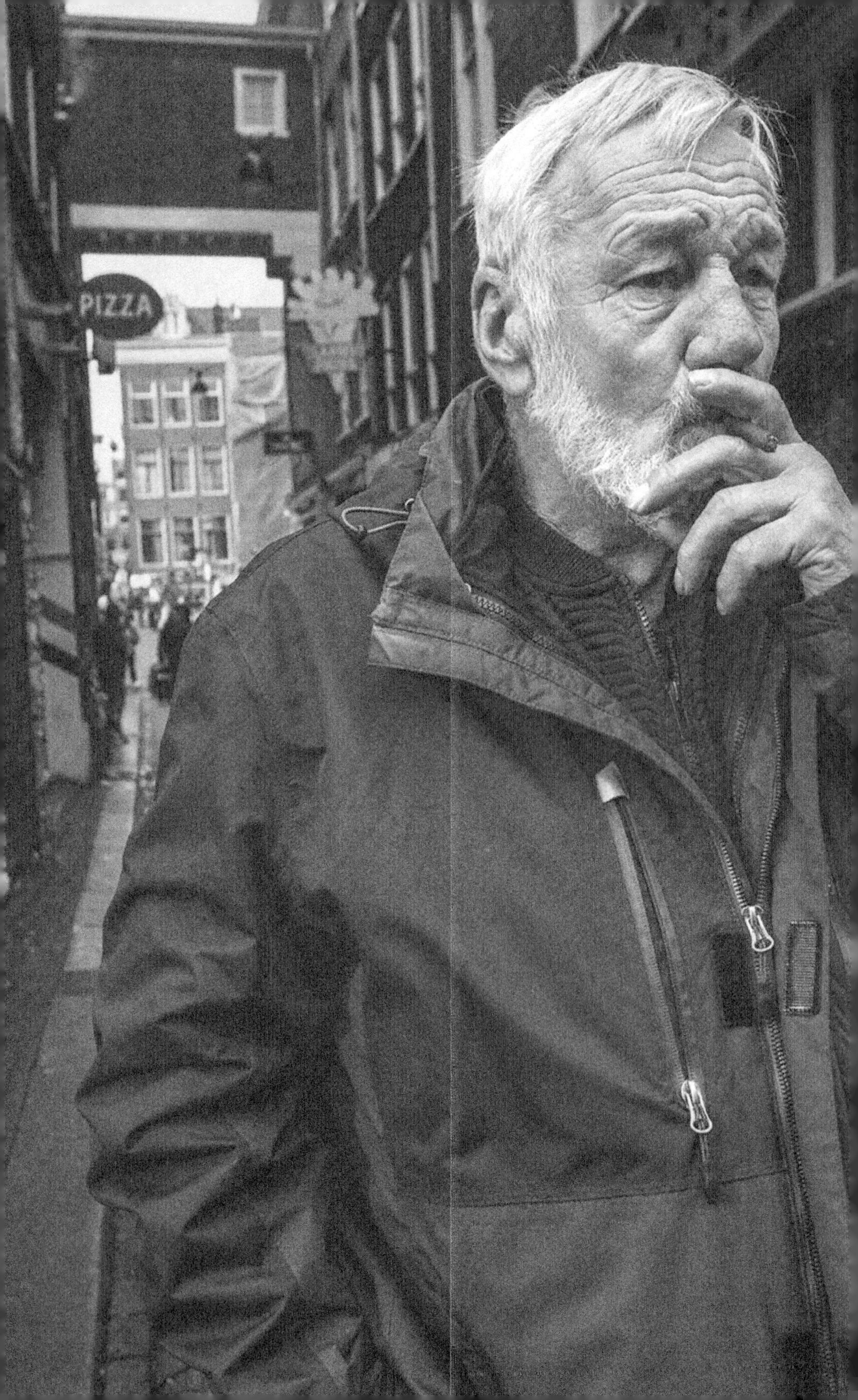
PIZZA

I think it's dumb that there isn't a police station anymore. That's something I would have protested against. By getting rid of it there is a lot more distance created between police and the neighbourhood. Luckily the community police officer is back again, but if it's enough I don't know? The police have to be in closer contact with the people, making sure that certain things can't happen and not shifting the responsibility to city inspectors. I wonder if the people who have to do that work can even handle it".

Joep pauses to take a couple of bites of his apple pie. It gives us both a moment to reflect. A bit of whipped cream is stuck in his beard. "It's another era," he continues. "There is a different kind of person living here now. More educated than before and who isn't so interested in the old neighbourhood. They are looking for an appropriate living space in the most beautiful part of Amsterdam. After the war we had a lot of artists in the neighbourhood. They were often alternative types who looked for space in a community where people were a little laid back, where you were free to mess around a bit. In Amsterdam-Zuid people were more likely to make comments than here where people didn't pay much attention to you. There were more possibilities here and you were left alone. That attracted a certain public. You for instance, but also me. The older residents are slowly disappearing.

People also had trouble with each other before, but you could resolve it easier because everyone knew everyone else. People are less tolerant towards each other these days. They don't want to hear the noise from the pub next door and they don't want to be bothered by the tourists on the street. People find themselves terribly important. I think that's a general shift in society.

Everyone experiences nuisance differently. Look at the Zeedijk in the past! Every pub had the door open, what an infernal racket. But the neighbourhood didn't complain about it. If you lived there you opened your window and set down a cushion hoping to see a good fight. Your sister cleaned the pub so you had nothing to say about it. That sort of interdependence is slowly fading. The biggest problem is the idea that anything goes in Amsterdam. You see visitors doing things here that they would never do in their own country. Travelling is too easy and much too cheap. That's why it's so busy here. I think that a tourist comes to Amsterdam because we have a beautiful city. They go to the

Rijksmuseum and the Anne Frank House, but they also want to see the Wallen. It is one of the attractions. The only bad thing is that the influx is just too much. Venice and Barcelona have the same problems. You can't control it anymore. That is really not nice for the people who live here in the neighbourhood. All the gawkers are driving some women I know behind the windows completely crazy, but I think it's hard to do something about that. Do you have to put up fences? Signs saying 'the neighbourhood is full come back tomorrow'? I know that that you don't agree, but I think that it's really an indication that window prostitution has had its day. The windows don't have to shut down in my opinion, but maybe it's not such a bad idea to relocate them. I had suggested moving them on a big cargo ship in the IJ or maybe even better: a luxurious four-star cruise ship. Also throw that idea for an erotic hotel in there and you're done with all the bullshit".

After the last bite of pie Joep finally wipes the whipped cream from his beard. We say goodbye and he leaves whistling, like always. Just like everyone remembers him. Every junkie and dealer used to be able to hear him from a distance and could quickly vacate to a corner further up. To me a Wallen without window brothels and fringe elements would really feel like a house that wasn't lived in. Like a kitchen where no one cooks because they're afraid of making a mess. Joep is right in saying that I don't agree with him. I like experimenting, but shutting the windows with the promise of opening them somewhere else, that's something I have very little faith in. Besides, if the problem is the overcrowding and visitor's behaviour and not window prostitutes, then that's what needs to be tackled. It's no excuse to say that that's more difficult achieve.

> "It is 1990. I haven't been working for a while. This time it's for good. Although, never say never. But I think that I am really done with the work. There wasn't really a moment where I thought: I'm stopping now. I can hardly remember the last day anymore. It happened over time. You gradually lose interest in it. Then I was earning less and less until finally you think: what am I still doing this for? I have to clean up some of my own internal clutter, if I can put it that way, and then I have to decide what I will do. A normal job doesn't interest me. I try a few things but I get bored too fast and I am not good at working for a boss

anyway. I start my own business and occupy myself with the only subject that I really understand: prostitution. People are shocked when I talk about it. But why? I want to change that. I feel a growing need to explain and educate. I am aware of the impact it will have on the rest of my life if I choose to be open about it. Some people avoid me or they are disgusted by me. I hadn't noticed that before. Others find it mostly fascinating but still keep me at a distance. Luckily, my real friends don't have a problem with it. I have a boyfriend who is too sweet and stupidly I trade him in for an idiot. Before I can – after a long time and a lot of trouble – get out of that, he calls me a whore. I am floored. How long has he been keeping that to himself'?

We cross to the other side and visit the Sint Annenkwartier, an area that has changed the most in the last ten years. First we go into the Dollebegijnensteeg. Searching for an explanation for this cute street name, I find a wonderful story written by a school teacher about one hundred and fifty years ago. In it he explains the name of the alley through a citation issued in 1629, where it's clear 'what kind of women' the street was already known for: 'And it appears from the public citation, that it was rightly a drunkard's alley then, where "great insolence and mischief was practised by those who frequented the local inns". (...) Those dolle begijnen (mad Beguines) have probably been around from the sixteenth century, or if not, then from before. And we will try to discover, what sort of women we are to understand the name refers to. (...) Thus, the Dollebegijnensteeg has had a bad reputation already from long ago, and was, even in the seventeenth century, as noted in the above citation, barely advanced in it's path to moral improvement".

The Sint Annenkwartier is made up of five streets and a covered area known as the Passage. It is a small area sandwiched between the Warmoesstraat and the Oudezijds Voorburgwal, near the Wijde Kerksteeg. It was a popular area when all of the window brothels were still operating and especially busy evenings and weekends. Even now, although most of the windows are shut down, there are still hundreds of people trying to squeeze through the narrow Trompettersteeg in the evenings. When global tourism was growing, but still hadn't reached today's levels and the tax department had other priorities, there was a lot of money being made in the whole neighbourhood and the Sint Annenkwartier topped them all. It was at this time that I got to know Jamila. She worked in the Trompettersteeg. I always thought she was one of the most beautiful women in the neighbourhood; long black hair and big dark eyes with eyelashes that touched the sky. She had a suspicious but charming boyfriend with pimp aspirations. Something I was familiar with.

"I know that I was pretty good looking, but I didn't think about it then. It's too bad that I didn't take more advantage of that", she says laughingly while we have a coffee and talk about the old days. "Although I have mixed feelings because it was also a really difficult time. My first year I worked in the Bloedstraat. Most of what I made went to Murat, my boyfriend who was much shorter than me and four years younger by-the-way. I used a lot of coke and I was in love. Then you don't think about it. I worked hard and brought some of the money to the bank. It was busy. I once calculated that I earned a hundred thousand guilders in the first year that I worked.

I didn't have any problem with the work. Behind the window I was the boss. I felt strong and powerful and I was free to do as I pleased. No one could touch me. It was a challenge and a nice change of pace. My whole family knew what I did and it was nice not to have to lie about it. A double life is nothing for me, it would destroy me. I was also always honest with my mother about my drug use. I don't ever want to hide who I am and what I do. You accept it or you don't, with all the problems that come with it. I dumped Murat once I figured out that I wasn't the only one. He left after a serious confrontation, where I broke a couple of ribs, taking all my savings. I moved from the Bloedstraat to the Trompettersteeg. I was rid of him, I worked for myself and so I didn't have those long days anymore. I wanted to make enough to be able to live and to keep using coke. Unfortunately that was my weak spot. The thought of how much money I made is really nuts. As fast as it came in, it was gone again – sadly. I have nothing to show for it and these days I have to get by on fifty euro a week. Yes indeed, different times. Luckily we didn't have to pay taxes then. I wouldn't have never been able stay on top of the bookkeeping. The girls that I hung around with in the neighbourhood were just as young as me and led, shall we say, lives that were not so structured.

I didn't have any contact with colleagues who were more serious about their work, but they were certainly around. Across from me in the alley someone worked in a window that I looked out on. She was older than me and worked very professionally. I thought about that once in a while. She had a lot of regular clients. She was someone who would be fine nowadays with all that accounting and stuff. I had a couple of regulars but not many. I was much too impatient for that and I wasn't interested in them enough".

Drugs caused a lot of problems in her life. "Didn't it make you vulnerable and blinded to what was going on?", I ask. "Well, it was just my work and my life at that moment," Jamila says. "I had a problem with that boyfriend, but I have never felt like a victim. Not even when I was giving him all my money. I knew pretty well what I was doing and I fixed it. What do I think is important? Good control and safety. To me self-control is more important than government control. I have always felt safe in my work everywhere because I worked in places where there was good contact with the landlord. That's the first one who comes if something happens. The police are always too late or not in the area. There was always someone from the rental office around and I could go to them personally if I had a problem. I have had particularly good experiences with female managers. You know, we aren't so quick to go to the police. You seek support from each other. Anyway, in my time going to the police was 'not done'. The Wallen is like a village. In between clients I would often go and get a sandwich from the Lunchroom here on the corner of the Oudekerksplein. There was always someone there who you would stop and chat with. In my work it was never about the sex. It was about the life around that and the friendly atmosphere in the neighbourhood. I still miss that".

> "It is 2007. The city is holding a press conference in Hotel Krasnapolsky. We have been hearing rumours for some time now. They have all kinds of plans for the Wallen. People look with suspicion to the neighbourhood since the negative report on prostitution in Amsterdam by Karina Schaapman appeared. Totally by coincidence, Mayor Cohen, Lodewijk Asscher and Els Iping announce with a lot of fanfare and fancy words that they want to clean up the Wallen. Asscher waves the

report from Schaapman around as proof of everything that's wrong. I already saw that coming. Criminals will be dealt with, brothel owners bought out, and sub-standard businesses will have to make room for high quality businesses. Windows have to shut down and poor women saved. I sit listening in a back corner with the steam coming out of my ears. I don't get it and find it all blown out of proportion. Why go through it with a bulldozer? Of course there are things that could be improved, but you have laws for that, don't you? And isn't there such a thing as consulting with each other? This seems more like a declaration of war with the battle being waged over the backs of the women that they say they want to help".

For the moment there are still red lights in parts of the Trompettersteeg and the rest of the Sint Annenkwartier. It's not clear right now what will happen here in the future. Probably it will depends on how much money the city has available to buy out brothel owners or to proceed with litigation. Or maybe they will let it deliberately and slowly fall into decay. A shame, because this area is actually a perfect location for window prostitution. You could even experiment with banning tourist groups and making it more attractive for sex workers and clients again. However, the majority of windows have been closed in the last few years and replaced by other kinds of businesses. Different, but then again not. In a place where there was once a brothel, tourists can now have their picture taken as a window prostitute. Not long after other locations were shut down you could find artists making red light inspired art and fashion. In the meantime various businesses have located here and even a supermarket. Surrounding the remaining window brothels is now a hodgepodge of this, that and everything. Nothing against the business owners but the whole atmosphere feels like it's trying too hard, as if conceived by someone from behind a desk. Enforced change by the city in an effort to 'upgrade' the neighbourhood at the expense of a group of people they don't want around anymore. The people responsible will just shrug their shoulders about this. If someone experiences something as painful, that's part of the gentrification process.

The buildings that border the opposite side of the Sint Annenstraat make up part of the Blaauwlakenblok; a cluster of historical buildings

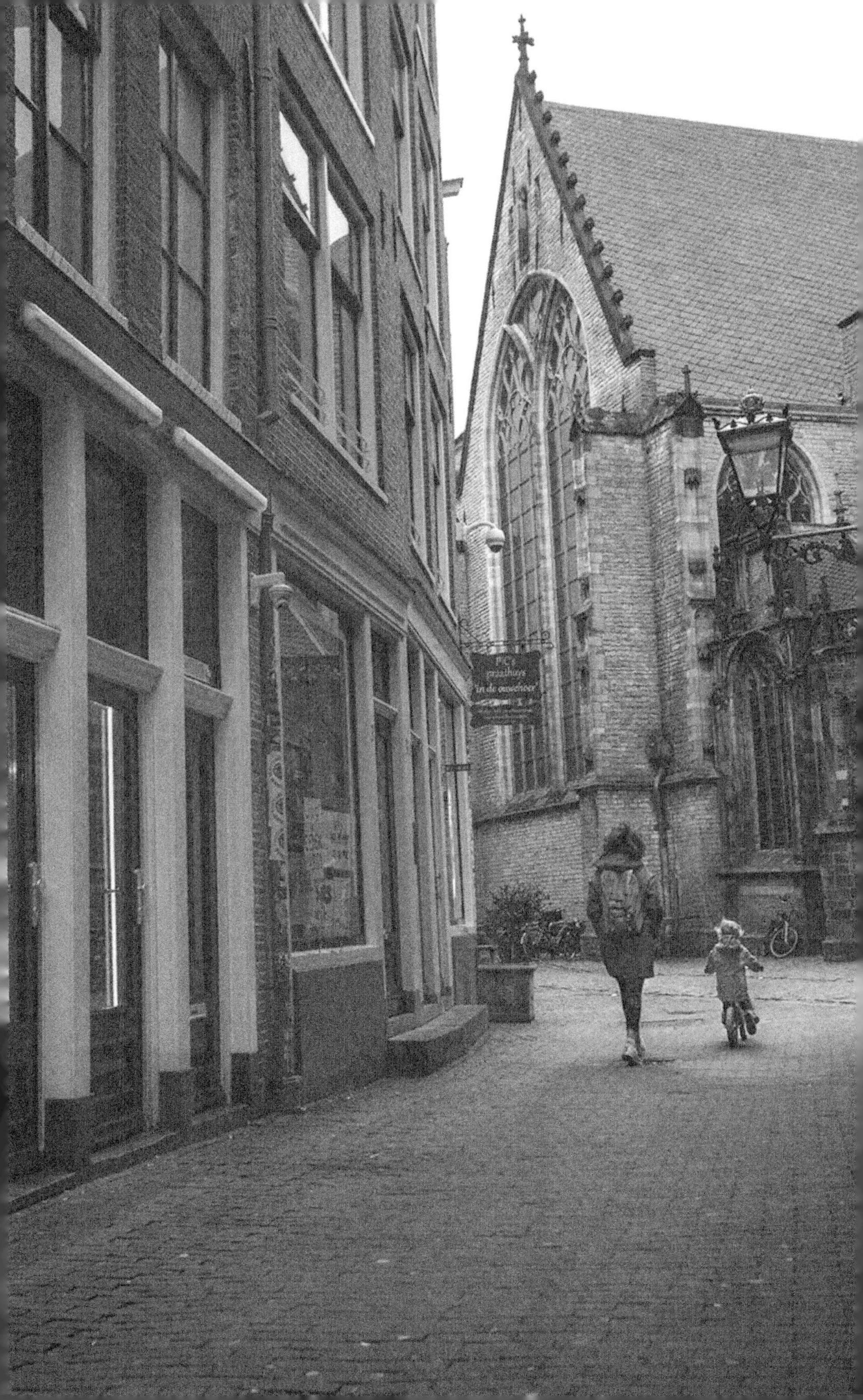

that extends right to the Sint Jansstraat. For years it was occupied by squatters and had become really dilapidated, until around 2002 when extensive renovations began after decades of legal wrangling. A number of families live in the 'blok', including Theodoor and Marijke's family. Theodoor and Marijke are the owners of the famous Condomerie in the Warmoesstraat. "Without young people there is no future for the Wallen," Theodoor says when I ask what it's like to live here with children and where they could play safely outside when they were still small. "Around twenty years ago, during the renovation of the Blaauwlakenblok, I really fought for more play space here," he continues. "There were fifty-five children living here at the time. I didn't get any support from city officials. The city didn't give any thought to it then and actually they still don't.

It was already impossible for children to play in the Warmoesstraat when our kids were still young. Marijke and I transformed an outside space in our block into an outdoor gym for them to play in. They would also play tennis behind the Bijenkorf department store. When the Blaauwlakenblok was being renovated they played in buildings on the Oudezijds Voorburgwal that had been stripped empty. That was really exciting for them. Every day our children had to cross through the neighbourhood to go to school. We called the sex workers 'kiss madams'. My son told me that he later dealt with his discomfort by focussing on the middle of the street when he walked past the windows. Afternoons we let the children take a detour via the Damstraat to avoid the busyness of the Wallen. Recently at a meeting about the neighbourhood, my daughter Ava said that she felt safe in the Wallen. Another girl, a neighbour from the Sint Jansstraat, said the same. When the city representatives who were there heard this, they almost fell in shock from their chairs".

Just about everyone I talk to who grew up here says that they felt safe in the neighbourhood as a child. That is in direct contrast to what people think and assume in the 'outside world'. You also see a difference between children who live and feel at home here and children who visit with their parents or come on a school trip to the Wallen. The women behind the windows really don't appreciate the latter. These children don't know how they should behave here and this actually makes it even more uncomfortable for both parties.

Ferry lives on the corner of the Sint Annenstraat en Sint Annendwarsstraat. He worked for a window brothel owner and a few years ago he moved, along with the company's window brothels, to the Singel area. Before he got this job, he ran errands for the window prostitutes in the neighbourhood. He did that for more than ten years. "You can earn good money", Ferry says when we bump into him on the Oudekerksplein. "I would always go home with a decent amount in tips. The girls need all kinds of things when they are at work: food, drinks, condoms, sponges, dildo's, you name it. I wasn't the only one who ran errands. You had Willem and Daan, old Rob and young Rob and they all had their own little turf. There's no one anymore now. The economy has changed, earnings are lower; it's another time. They do their own shopping now. There was also old uncle Chris, he was there too. He would go and get coffee for someone and if she was busy and the curtains were closed when he came back, he could never find her again. We told him: 'Write it down then,' but he refused to do that. 'I worked for years in restaurants, I'm perfectly capable at remembering an order,' he'd say.

The Sint Annenkwartier was my turf. I made sure that I always had change and I gave out my telephone number. That way they could call me if they needed anything and I advanced the costs. One of the women around the corner here paid me twenty-five guilders to vacuum the stairs. No problem, I did it. Once I had to get champagne and snacks for someone because she was throwing a goodbye party in her room and it was her last day. A week later she was back again.

It was really easy money here. One time I asked a woman who stood looking a bit angry behind the window, what the matter was. Then she said: 'I only made a thousand guilders today.' I really had to explain to her that that's not normal. After that period I continued happily living here at the corner for another nine years. It's busy, but I have never had much trouble with sleeping and such. It was mostly difficult when I had to let the dog out. I had a big German Shepherd that I named Joep, after the neighbourhood policeman. One time there was a British guy standing freaking out under my window. Joep was already waiting on the stairs, ready to go out. By the time the police came running this way, the guy was trapped in a corner. Yep, that dog was a pretty handy.

I rent out the rooms for my work. If there is a problem, then I go and deal with it or call the police. It's a very different atmosphere in the Singel area where our windows are now. It's quieter. There are more Dutch clients and also older sex workers. It's a really different public on the street than in the Wallen. Now instead of a German Shepherd I have a little mutt. In that neighbourhood it's really enough".

> "It is 1984. I am working together with a friend in a hostess bar on the Nieuwendijk, under-the-table. It's a snack bar during, day selling mostly hotdogs, and evenings it's a club where the DJ stands naked and I earn ten guilders for every glass of fake champagne that a client buys me. We call it a piccolo and for me it's 7-up with a drop of blue dye. Nothing much happens. Dancing and fooling around a bit, nothing more. We sleep behind a bed sheet hung in the living room of the owner's house on the Warmoesstraat, above the Madame Arthur bar and around the corner from the Sint Annenstraat. Sometimes we are allowed to go down to the bar to watch the drag queens perform. The bar is often packed and it's dark and hazy from the smoke. I love it. La Michelle lipsyncs her songs from the stool on the tiny stage and I watch her breathlessly. We always have to scurry quickly back upstairs because if the police come there will be big trouble. We are still underage and the boss doesn't want to take any risks. The atmosphere in the neighbourhood draws me in like a magnet. I'm not familiar with the Wallen around the corner yet. But that's just a question of time".

In the Ziggy cafe we get into conversation with 'de Kleine Bokser' (the Little Boxer), who I know from the old neighbourhood when we were both quite a bit younger. "I am from the Jordaan," he says to me. "I was twelve or so when I discovered the Wallen and came here together with my brother when we were on our way to the Waterlooplein. It was the seventies. Of course the the neighbourhood was very interesting for young boys. When I grew up here there were a lot more sex shops and there was one woman working here who I thought was pretty exciting. I kept trying to find her again, but usually I just got lost".

He has the same Jordaans accent as Tonia. Today's old guard residents and business owners are all real Amsterdammers who have lived and worked almost their entire lives in the Wallen. They have so many stories and experiences and play an essential role in preserving the social fabric of the area, what Laurens Buijs discussed. With the passing of just a little more time they will be replaced by a new generation, most of whom have no connection to the neighbourhood.

"With open arms the city has welcomed big money into the area with the position that criminal real estate holdings have to be taken away from shady owners and sold on to legitimate parties. I wonder why the city is still talking about real estate being in the hands of criminals," de Kleine says sighing. "These days everything has to be screened through the Public Administration Anti-corruption Act, so if you're a criminal there is no way you will get anywhere. It's really very difficult to get rid of criminal money here in this neighbourhood anymore. Project 1012 has done a lot of things badly, but it's also led to some good things. One good thing is that foreign parties don't have any interest in real estate here anymore because of the added controls around buying property.

There's a lot less trouble in the neighbourhood these days. Except for it being really busy, but my apartment has double glazing everywhere so it doesn't bother me much. It was busy in the old days too and on top of that, it was packed with parked cars along the canal. Everyone just drove through. There were junkies and dealers everywhere. It was even busy behind the windows on the cheap side of the canal. By every tree there were twenty men standing waiting for their turn for a cheap lay. When one went out, the next one went in. If someone who was stoned fell asleep behind the window we would toss fireworks down from upstairs. But that's all in the past. I was in youth gangs until I was eighteen. We fought a lot and stole Kreidler and Zundapp mopeds. There was someone here in the neighbourhood who bought them from us. I would also hang around a lot at the snack bar in the Stoofsteeg or at the Torenzicht cafe. I left all that nasty business behind the moment I got involved with someone and started earning money.

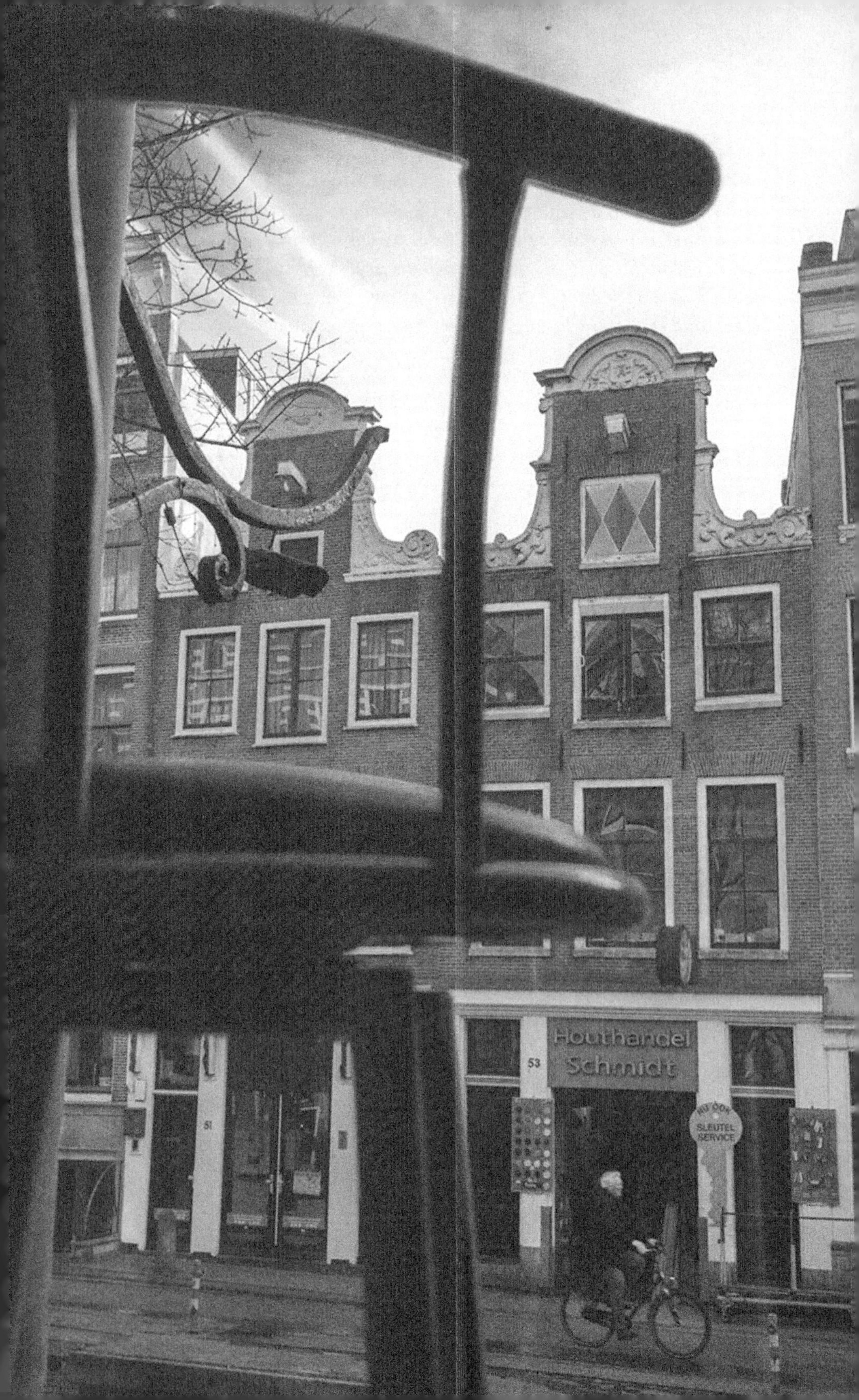
Houthandel
Schmidt
53
51
SLEUTEL
SERVICE

In the early-eighties everything was for sale. You could buy buildings on and around the Zeedijk for six thousand guilders. The junkies came free with your purchase. No one believed that anything good would ever come of the neighbourhood. In the meantime a lot has improved. I own some real estate in the Wallen and I also live there. The city and the papers like to keep going on about criminals in the Wallen, but seriously, they all left long ago. A criminal couldn't get a licence for anything and there is nowhere here where they could spend their money". "What about crime on the street," I ask. "There aren't any pimps on the canal anymore so there is no control on the street either," de Kleine says. "You notice a rise in the nuisance caused by street dealers because no one goes after them. In the early days they were kicked off the street. The police make a round now and then, but they really only come when they're called and the city inspectors are busy giving people directions instead of doing something about the screaming British tourists and the dealers". "That not having a pimp isn't normal anymore is an improvement," I remark. "Come on a pimp, what is that really? To me a pimp is someone who handcuffs the girl to the radiator. Most of the girls just have a boyfriend, not a pimp. Back then the boyfriends came along to work and kept the streets clean and the girl safe. But if he comes now she won't get a room, so he stays away.

The best scenario is that the neighbourhood remains as it is and that the city's money goes toward rule enforcement. It's the least expensive solution to managing the crowds. The people who complain the loudest about 'the craziness in the Wallen' have probably never been to Times Square in New York. Now that's crowded. Or go to Delhi or Bangkok. We really have no idea here what crowded is. It will become even worse. People from China and India are going more and more on vacation. Amsterdam has worked hard on its popularity, continually saying 'come to Amsterdam'. Now everyone is coming and it's too busy again".

That's also what former brothel owner Tonia said in her story: "For years I have been a resident of the Wallen as well as a business owner. This is what I think when it comes to the discussion about how busy the Wallen is because of window prostitution: On the Leidseplein and the Rembrandtplein it's just as busy and there are no window brothels there. See, when I let the dog out at night I don't walk along the canal.

I know that it is too crowded to go for a walk, so I take the Beursstraat. I don't mind. It is busier than in the past. There are a lot of windows closed and the sex shops have to close at ten. The area where the tourists walk around, is a lot smaller than it was. They walk in a smaller area and very close to each other. Where I do have a problem is with all the drunk tourists getting wasted and vomiting on my doorstep. You can't do much about it because it happens mostly late at night and you don't see it".

"The people who visit the Wallen also go to other parts of the city," de Kleine continues. "It's nonsense to think that if you close the windows that it will be quieter here. That's not how it works. You have to enforce the rules in the places where it's really busy. That is the way it is everywhere. If you're drunk and stand screaming on Times Square, they just pick you up. Here you have four city inspectors standing on the bridge and no one does anything. No one wants to get their hands dirty. Before the guys from the neighbourhood did it, then there were some hard blows dealt out. That's not tolerated anymore. Now if you smack someone, you'll be arrested. Just put a police van in the middle of the bridge between the Molensteeg and the Oudekennissteeg. Then everyone sees that the police are in the area and will behave themselves. If someone does something, arrest them. Done and dusted. And if you don't want people to get so drunk, then you have to stop serving so much alcohol. Do something about it. In the past we were all one community and we took care of things together. The city has driven a wedge between people. That's gone. The people who own businesses in the Wallen these days are just business people. They have their permits and pay their taxes, but they are still seen as criminals regardless. The brothel controls here are the toughest that you can imagine. If there is still a criminal somewhere among them, the city is doing something wrong".

You don't just leave the Wallen. De Kleine echoes the feeling of many real Wallen residents: "I'll keep living in the neighbourhood as long as I can climb the stairs. Or I will have to install an elevator in my building. Then I'll stay forever; as long as there is double glazing".

"It is 1986. Luckily I have made rent already from two fifty guilder clients so the pressure is off. I did have to stand for a long time for that though. Things are quiet. There are enough people on the street, but it seems no one is interested in getting laid. My colleagues across from me don't have much to do either. Everyone hangs around somewhat annoyed, either sitting on the stool or dancing a little. Suddenly, I hear a scream and I see people running past towards the bridge. Breaking glass, shouting and a bunch of loud banging can only mean one thing: there's a fight. We open the door and look around the corner. In the meantime there is a traffic jam on the street because no one can get through. All the way at the front, by Yüksel, is a blue Mercedes. 'Oh oh', we say. Fred, my close colleague's husband, stands next to the car shouting. In one hand he's holding a cigar and has a baseball bat in the other. The boys are already running from the other side of the street. Within a minute a huge fight breaks out on the canal. All the girls are standing in their doorways. G is just about to run outside to help her man when we hear sirens. People scurry off in all directions. When the police come by the windows later to see if anyone saw anything, nobody has. The ranks close".

It has started getting windy and it's cold outside. The Oudekerksplein still looks barren after last spring's storm violently uprooted the hundred and fifty year old trees there. Belle looks a little lonely now that her natural guardians no longer protectively surround her. She stands near the Oude Kerk's tower next to a historical streetlamp. I always feel warmth and a lot of love when I see her. Belle is a statue made in honour of all sex workers and calls for respect. She was created by my aunt, artist Els Rijerse and is cast in bronze. Her posture is proud and strong. There are memorials held here, people come here to mourn and she is the start or end-point for demonstrations and gatherings of sex workers who are fighting for their rights. A group of tourists come and stand around Belle. Nice that she gets some attention. We walk past with a smile and stand for a moment by the entrance to the church tower.

I have a special connection with the Oude Kerk. Like all the buildings from the middle ages it's also a beautiful monument. It has seen a lot. Red light illuminates the walls into the darkest hours of the night. All the corners stink of urine in the mornings before it's cleaned to prevent damage to the stone. And yet, the walls have already survived eight hundred years and will probably still be standing in another eight hundred. Every Sunday morning there is a church service. You could say that it is quite extraordinary that a church is the physical centre point of the Wallen. I have always explained this to tourists with a great sense of pride. Don't be ashamed of what makes you unique. I hope the red light may shine on the church for a long while yet.

We walk through the Oudekerksplein past the Stones cafe and back to where we began. It's too cold now to sit outside. The cafe terraces on the square are empty except for a couple of smokers. Soon, in the summer, they'll be packed every day and well into the night by stag parties of drunk, hormonally beset men in pink tutus and shrieking English 'ladies'. The women who work next door will be stared at and commented on. A client has to be pretty brave to go in there. There was a time when the size of the terraces couldn't be increased and there was no desire for more bars and restaurants in the neighbourhood. There are really quite a lot of new bars and restaurants since Project 1012, mostly close to where the window brothels are.

We had parked our bikes near the PIC. I see that it is time to get some new plants for the planter by the front door and remind myself to bring some the next time I'm in the neighbourhood. The PIC plays an important role in the Wallen. That may not always be visible to everyone, but it does. For more than twenty five years now anyone who visits the Wallen can go there for any reason and with all their questions. The foundation struggles for more understanding, respect and social acceptance of sex workers and their work. Information is mainly provided by people with experience in the profession which means that the organisation is still unique in the world.

We wave to the women we still know behind the windows in the Enge Kerksteeg and at the end of the street I turn to look back. It is my favourite little alley with a view. Artist Anton Pieck once made a drawing of this alleyway and almost nothing has changed. The PIC sign hangs in almost the same place as the coffee and tea shop sign that hung there a hundred years ago.

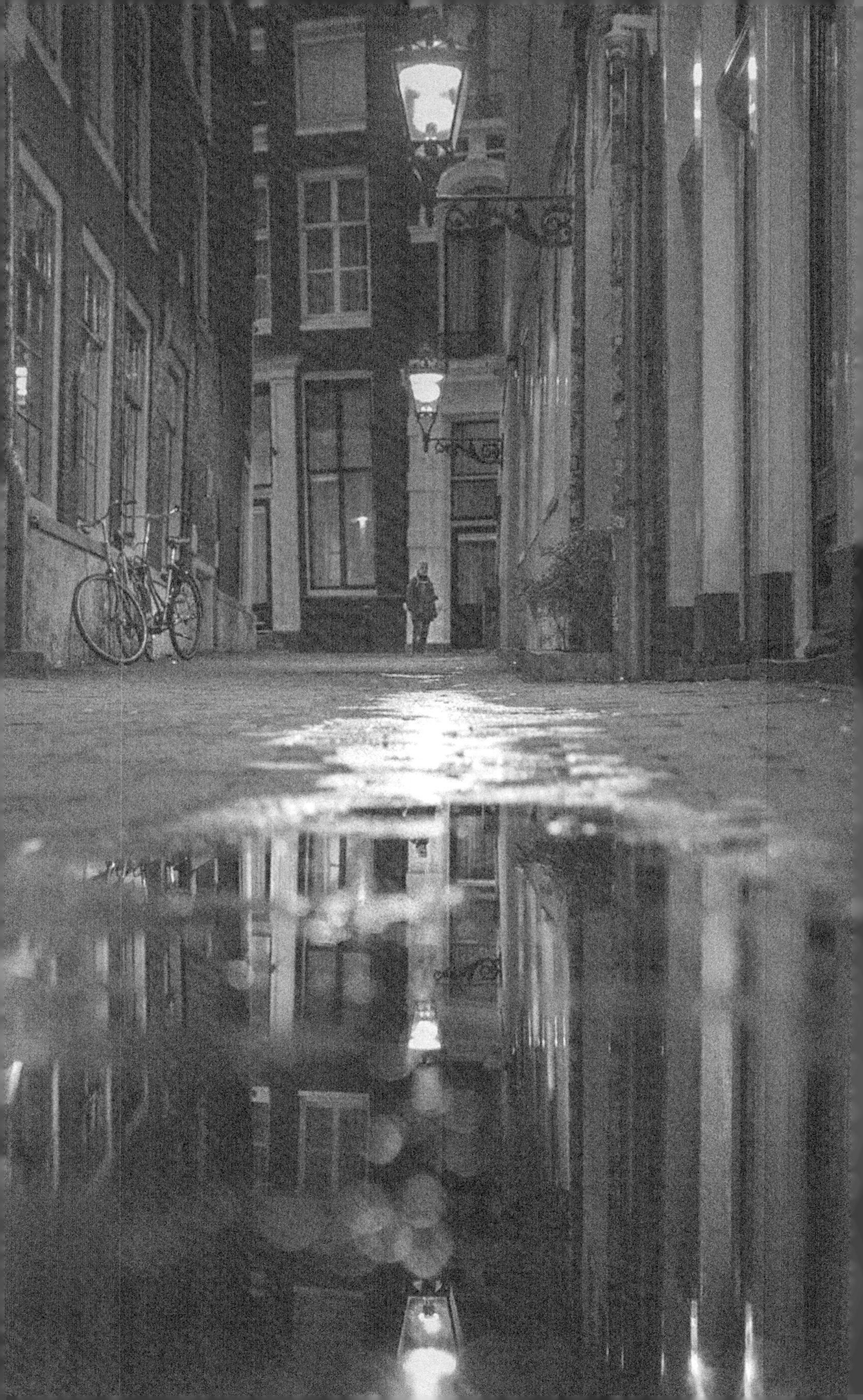

Do I romanticise the Wallen? Maybe I do. But it's a matter of how you see and experience things. I remember something Joep said today. He said that people feel attracted to the neighbourhood 'because you could mess around a bit.' For me that's firmly in the past. In a lecture, Marie-Louise Janssen, from the University of Amsterdam, once called the Wallen 'a (sexual) free-zone for alternative thinkers and free spirits, with an important symbolic and social function'. That really resonated with me when I heard it. A free-zone for alternative thinkers sounded like music to my ears. What I imagine by being 'alternative thinking' is that you won't be pigeonholed. That you follow your own path and that this is different from the social norm. Merging these two concepts captures, for me, the essence of the Wallen's allure and what I recognise in the people from the neighbourhood and our conversations. No, this is no place for holier-than-thou types. Although, thinking about the Oude Kerk, former convents and the hidden church Ons' Lieve Heer op Solder, we have enough of those too. And that is exactly what makes the Wallen what it is.

Our current Mayor's objectives sound nice, but how will they be achieved? Sex workers rights are a priority, just as resident's quality of life is. In our conversation she wondered 'if there was a way to kill two birds with one stone'. But maybe that is exactly what the starting point should be. Ensure that the Wallen remains a neighbourhood for everyone who is also a part of it now. Because it's all well and good, but sex workers are saying: 'This is our neighbourhood too'.

Mayor Halsema thinks that the Wallen without window brothels will still be the same. Waffle shop owner Shab, opts for another extreme and says that the Wallen without window brothels is like Paris without the Eiffel Tower. The answer to the question of whether window prostitution is still of this time and whether you want it to remain a part of the Wallen, depends simply on which perspective you choose. In her story, Anaisa said: "I have this neighbourhood and my work. If they take that away from me, that's when I'll need help". The future will reveal whether her message was heard or whether sex workers rights stop at the threshold to the window.

At the top of the Oude Brugsteeg we take a moment by the sex shop. The sign that helped Robin recognise that we had arrived in the Wallen doesn't hang there anymore. It had to go because it was too gaudy and didn't fit the city's new image of the neighbourhood. Now it's a bare and ugly piece of wall. I shake my head. Little by little it seems the area is being moulded into a socially and politically correct 'former rough neighbourhood'. Laurens Buijs made a comparison to Stockholm: "An historical city without a soul". He said: "One day all that you'll have here is only one mannequin sitting behind a window, with one red light that is supposed to represent the historic red light district". I hope that it doesn't come that far.

"It is 1996. I am lying on the sofa. Santa is dead. Yesterday she couldn't stand up anymore. She was done. My family came right away and we all went together to the veterinarian. Still in her dog bed, we lifted her up and set her in the back of the car. I laid beside her. I couldn't say goodbye and bawled my eyes out when the vet gave her the final lethal injection. We have been through so much together. I feel like I will never get over this loss. Then Willem calls me. With a big smile he asks me to come to the kitchen. To make him happy I had finally taken the pregnancy test that I had planned to take earlier this week. Triumphantly, He holds the test strip up and shows me the clear pink line. The sun breaks through. Robin is on her way".

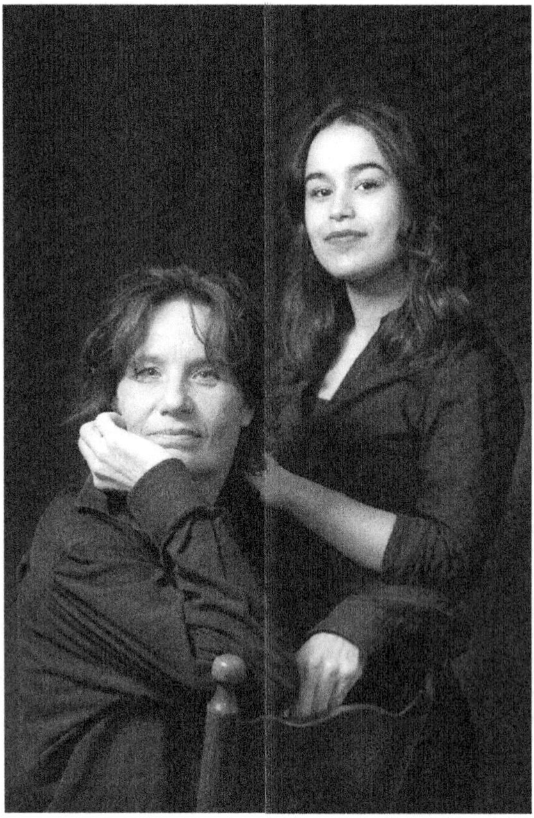

Sources

Over the last 25 years I have read and learned a lot about the Wallen. Next to my own personal experiences my knowledge about the area comes from various sources. The two most important of which are The Burgher and the Whore by Lotte van de Pol and Liefde te Koop [Love for Sale, Dutch only] by Annemarie de Wildt and Paul Arnoldussen.

Page 44-45: Soa Aids Nederland (2018). De Legale facade. Sekswerkbeleid: hoe kan het anders? [The Legal Facade. Sex work policy: how could it be different?]

Page 45: 'Duizenden slachtoffers van seksuele uitbuiting': Feit of frame? Tijdschrift voor seksuologie, 2019, Jaargang 43, nummer 2. [Thousands of victims of sexual exploitation: Fact or framing? Journal for sexology 2019, issue 43, no. 2]

I have cited the following websites:

www.onsamsterdam.nl and www.joodsamsterdam.nl regarding the Greyfriars Monastery and the Bloedstraat on page 67 and regarding the Zeedijk on page 40.

www.stadsarchief.amsterdam.nl regarding the pamphlet from 1908 about children in brothels on page 31.

www.velehanden.nl regarding the Dollebegijnensteeg on page 89.

Important Editor's Note:

This release is an Amazon print-on-demand version of our book. The images are therefore of a lower quality. Despite this they are integral to the story and we did not want you to miss them.

List of photographs

All of the images were made by Robin Haurissa

Page 3: Shadow on the Oude Kerk
Page 10: Steps in front of the PIC
Page 12: Nigel the window washer
Page 18: Warmoesstraat
Page 25: Korte Niezel
Page 27: Korte Niezel
Page 34: Oudezijds Achterburgwal
Page 38: Mayor Femke Halsema
Page 41: Stormsteeg
Page 48: Oudezijds Achterburgwal
Page 52: Oudezijds Voorburgwal
Page 55: Evert
Page 58: Jan and Monique
Page 61: Mariska in 'vacation window'
Page 63: Pussy behind the window
Page 69: Bloedstraat
Page 74: Geldersekade
Page 79: Enge Kerksteeg
Page 86: Joep de Groot
Page 93: Enge Kerksteeg
Page 98: Window Oudezijds Achterburgwal
Page 103: Enge Kerksteeg
Page 106: Selfportrait Robin and Mariska
Page 107: Map by (grant)pa Jaap Majoor (www.jaapmajoor.nl)
Page 109: Enge Kerksteeg

Cover front: Belle, statue on Oudekerksplein
Cover back: Oudekerksplein

Printed in Great Britain
by Amazon